Sane Enough Insane Enough

Simple Answers to Life's Complex Questions

Sunil Jaiswani

notionpress.com

INDIA • SINGAPORE • MALAYSIA

ISBN 979-8-89233-615-4

Contents

Preface 5

1.   Happiness: Choice and Comparison 9

2.   The Random: The Odds in Favour 33

3.   Chaos: The Opportunity Cost. 55

4.   Money: How Much is Enough? 75

5.   Society: Your Truth or Mine? 97

6.   Mindset: Ideas vs Execution... 115

7.   Success: The Flip Side.. .133

8.   Social Media: The Information Overload. 155

9.   Generations: The Millennials and the Z 175

10. Fitness: The Body and the Mind.. 197

11. Politics: The New Normal. 215

12. The Future: AI, Humans and the Symbiosis 235

Preface

Life is a complex journey in a complex world. Not because it's inherently like that, but because it's us, the beings, which make it complex with our views, beliefs, and actions, and sometimes intentionally for our own selfish purposes.

There isn't anything in this book that you didn't know earlier, but it's an attempt to simplify your thought process regarding various aspects of life, which we all wish should've been simpler and more peaceful to sail through.

What makes it difficult, though, is the mountain of available information with which it sometimes becomes impossible to choose between the right and wrong and the necessary from redundant.

It's time that we figure out that, in the case of 'information', the more we have isn't always better.

Also, life may not always work in accordance with what you have planned for yourself based on that available information, for there are a lot of forces and random factors at work to create a certain event, and the end result of our efforts isn't always in our hands despite taking the best of informed and calculated decisions.

Also, as we start, do know that keeping it simple is not akin to avoiding the complex but rather knowing what can and what cannot be solved, where to allocate your energy and where not to, and at the end breaking the complex into several simples if at all you wish to not move ahead without getting all the answers.

It also tries to make you aware that it's sometimes better to not have answers to all your questions and still be at peace with it, move on for better things in life, and still be thankful for that experience for the lessons it taught you.

Most of what the book has comes from my experience with people, relationships, and situations, and since it is the experiences that make a person in its entirety, it is what taught me that keeping it simple is the only way that remains to be at peace with the self and the noise of the world.

Although the book poses more questions than it answers, mainly because it is only you who can answer those queries for yourself depending on your experiences in life and your belief systems. There is no single absolute truth for everyone while there can still be a path or a thought process that will take you towards your 'truth' and what you want to do with it.

Why did I write this book in the first place? Probably because I've always wanted to. Also, because I speak less in general, so the book remains to be the only option to get my thoughts across to everyone.

Different individuals have different experiences and thought processes, and you may not agree with all of what someone else has learned through their own adventures. But if you read all of it, you would know that the book doesn't want you to agree to what it says and asks; all it wants you to do is to keep it simple and know that sometimes it's the only approach that can help you decipher the complex.

Let's Explore More…

1
Happiness

Does always chasing happiness make you unhappy?
And is it even possible to be happy all the time?

Have you sometimes wondered why some people appear happier than others even after seemingly having no reasons for it, or why some people are not happy even after having everything that you think can ever be wished for?

Someone rich and famous once said, "That you can still be unhappy comes as a shock when you have accomplished everything you ever dreamed of."

Is there a reason why we are not forever happy? Or we possibly are, and we just don't realise it, probably because we want to be happier.

A life puzzle is made of various pieces, and even if most aspects of our lives are almost perfect, you will be affected by the nuances of life on a regular basis based on your interactions with people and information consumed.

The emotions or the state of happiness remain to be the most wished for by our race, yet only a few people can figure out and attain that constant state of mind for a long duration of time. Though everyone wants to stay happy forever, it still means different things for different people, and on top of it, the meaning of it keeps changing with our experiences and age.

But if it's the same thing that everyone wants, why do they take such complex routes to reach there when it sounds so simple? And why are we not even satisfied when we reach our goals and achieve whatever we have always wanted to?

While we continuously want more out of our lives, our perception of happiness, based on the information of what is happening around us and in the world, makes us believe that we would be better off in some other situation or opportunity at this very moment than the one we are in. Also, that we deserve a lot more than what we have right now and achieving that may make us reach the extent of happiness that we are looking for.

That very something that can make us happier than we are right now is what we keep looking for all the time and sometimes too hard at it to lose a sense of the present and indulge in redundant things like pondering over uncertainties and the fear of the future or a regret from the past.

We feel that the state of unhappiness or discontent can only be cured when we will have more money, power, and comfort than we have right now. The mind keeps wanting something or the other.

When was the last time you remember not wanting anything?

Whether it's as small as some new dress, despite having an almirah full of them, or something like more respect and authority from your peers because you think you deserve it. The thought of how things should have been in your life as per what you think of your achievements, potential and stature and what you deserve as per your self-imagined way of life, is what keeps our thoughts occupied most of the time.

Even when we have the object of our desires, we might not experience a sustained increase in happiness from that moment. Instead, we often replace that thought process and continue pursuing the next things we want to do and achieve. It's a never-ending process given the number of things we could desire and the life situations we could really want to happen.

Emotions like love, sadness, anger, fear, and all else need a certain setup to exist and reduce in intensity or cease to exist altogether when these preconditions fade away or scenarios change with time. And with the changed conditions, any of those emotions must take another form and validation from the people involved to move onto its next phase.

And that's why it isn't always wise to take long-term decisions based on short-term emotions and impulses at any age.

All emotions require effort to overcome, except for the happy state of mind, which we aspire to maintain indefinitely. Unlike other emotions, it doesn't need any additional external events or efforts to fade away; it naturally diminishes over time.

And that, precisely, remains the greatest irony of humankind.

You cannot be happy and ecstatic for the same reason repeatedly, even if the setup and conditions remain the same, while you can stay sad or disappointed forever or for a prolonged period of time over a single reason or incident.

Our bodies and minds are wired in such a way that we can often live in a constant state of dissatisfaction, finding reasons to feel unsettled or incomplete despite being satisfied with many aspects of life.

The truth is that we all experience negative emotions at all stages of life, sometimes even multiple times a day. That's just a part of who we are and how the mind works, and nothing can change that.

There is also something strange about emotions; a variety of them surface at random times, sometimes even confusing us with their intensity.

And sometimes, random emotions also arise in response to events whose outcomes will not affect us in the present or in the future. That feeling of attachment when we don't even have a remote inclusion in the outcome but just the inclination of the heart to want a certain thing sometimes produces the most intense form of emotions.

Take an example of the 2023 World Cup final between India and Australia, considering India is a cricket-crazy nation and the team had reached the finals on their home turf; everyone wanted it to lift the World Cup that day.

But as it happened, they couldn't. And the team that played better on that day won. But it left everyone in a state of shock and heartbreak. It was so intense that even the people who aren't much interested in the sport couldn't stop feeling sad about it.

Could it have been for the pride of the nation, or the collective will of over a billion people, all aligned toward a common goal? The result, in either way, would not have affected anyone or their lives, but still, the emotions attached to the sport, the players, and the country took the better of everyone.

And a few months later, when the same team triumphed in the T20 World Cup final in 2024, the euphoria was overwhelming. The people were on the streets not only celebrating the current win but also the relief from the previous loss.

Sometimes the emotions are impulsive and random, sometimes for a reason, but it's good to believe that it's good to embrace them as they come because it's the way we are made.

Most people on the planet are dissatisfied for different reasons in and beyond their control. Still, they continue to strive hard in search of happiness and peace, sometimes even in things which are remotely connected to the feeling of it for it may bring them the feeling that they have been looking for.

Also, there isn't something called ultimate or continuous happiness; rather, it remains to be a state of mind or an emotion like all other emotions which takes place in bursts at certain times for a certain period in our lives. And if somehow you manage a state of life so that it was the only emotion in your life all day long and forever, with the absence of other emotions like fear, pain, and sadness, you wouldn't be able to recognise the difference in your being at all and would start searching for a better version or more intense form of happiness in some time.

There is very little value in things we have in excess in our lives; the moment we have a lot of anything, its significance goes for a toss. Similarly, the devaluation of a situation or emotion arises from the abundance of it in your lives.

The more you have of something, the more you neglect the current value of it and start looking for ways to get hold of more of it or something else, something better or unknown that may make you feel better. You start to try different things and experiments so as to be able to find your path that will align you to the path of ultimate happiness that you have always yearned for, irrespective of the fact that it may just be the same empty feeling you will be staring at, at the end of that tunnel.

But it still makes sense that if you don't like something in your life, do not keep wishing for it to change; do something about it, carefully though, because it's the emotional dissatisfaction during comfortable times due to which we make negligent decisions that can cause a lot of damage. And when everything has gone wrong due to the haste of it, we realize that it was not what we actually wanted, wishing we could go back to our previous life again.

Choice

Shouldn't having more choices imply better possibilities as per our customised requirements and result in better decision-making? And shouldn't we be alright having so many options to choose from as per our liking?

Since it allows us to go through every detail of all the available options and choose what suits us the best and not be satisfied only with what's the only available, like the earlier times when there were fewer or no choices.

Well, it's a paradox, more for the current world than it was a few decades back.

The freedom of choice sometimes will lead us anxious and frustrated, and later dissatisfied in the form of comparison of the final choice with the options we did not chose. Since the abundance of the options makes us go through all the details for the sake of taking a better decision that wouldn't otherwise matter much. More choices bring in more analysis and calculations with it.

Earlier, there were only a few variations of everything that we needed and could use, and we were not bombarded with thousands of choices when having to make a certain decision.

But that was also the time when we had to make do with what was available, and which was probably not the best. It brings us to the conundrum of choice, which says more and more options being easily available to us is a concern in more ways than one.

It also applies to the freedom of choice that we are allowed to have in terms of the choice of career, food, location, entertainment, clothing, or anything else.

Compare it with the times when we keep looking for content to watch on Netflix, scrolling through the infinite number of options while not being able to make up our minds, which a lot of times results in watching nothing at all.

The same applies to supermarkets, restaurants, or anything similar having a multitude of options for us to choose from. Having a lot of choice puts us under immense pressure to make an informed choice, the best one for that matter which cites our incapability if we still fall short of making a perfect choice out of the available options.

It's not that you only have to decide which option is the best in general but also that which one remains to be the best for you. It's just that your emotions allow your possible choices to vary impulsively as per the availability of what you want, the effort or the amount you are willing to invest, and the perspective of what that choice will result in.

You decide and move to the store to check out the options available, and what you see is that for every single choice of feature you have for a certain potential purchase, there are multiple options available that more or less wouldn't make a dent in the budget decided. While still being perplexed over the information available, you decide to go ahead with one.

Out of the multitude of options, you end up choosing some and regret not being able to choose or have some since you only had to buy one of them. What follows is regret and dissatisfaction and leads to self-blame of not being able to decide well when the choice made doesn't turns out to be a good one.

The presence of so many choices make it hard for us to decide, leading to decision anxiety and dissatisfaction.

In fact, it's observed that having more choices sometimes results in no decision being made at all, and often leads to poor choices as well.

Whenever you are making a choice to do something, you are also making a choice to not do something, and that's where the opportunity cost of everything not done comes in.

And since the very nature of that involves comparison of things we have to the things we could not, reduces the satisfaction of the results even if we have made an almost perfect decision with the information and choice available.

Comparisons at all stages of life with what we could not and cannot buy and have, with what we could've done better, and how life would've been if we were able to make a certain number of choices that we couldn't because of circumstances or limitations always maintain a space in our minds. And while the regrets that comes with small choices and decisions fades away, it's sometimes with the major decisions of life that turn wayward we tend to think if we could've made better choices along the way or could've taken more time doing it.

Also, as the number of decisions to be made increases, not solely because of more options but also wanting to do many things at once, the qualities of those decisions and the executions decline visibly.

Whenever we make a decision, the effect of subconsciously delaying it or not wanting to make one altogether to cause regret later is already factored in, which makes the whole process slower than it should be, which in turn also affects the quality of the original decision in the first place.

To add to it, we also tend to overestimate the regret factor when the result varies even by only a minor margin. If we miss a flight by an hour, it may cause lesser regret than missing the check-in process by just five minutes and not being allowed to travel. Not buying that model of a car that just costs only a bit more is more regretful than ruining your thoughts over the one that costs a lot more. Sometimes it does become a play of the margins.

There is no optimal course of action that can help us make the best decision that wouldn't make us feel bad on any level or in the future. It pans out how it's supposed to, at its own pace, exactly how it is with everything else in life.

A bigger choice related to career, marriage, life thus becomes a lot more difficult as going even a bit wrong with it can have big ramifications, as the mind will suggest and keep giving you reasons to delay the decisions in search for better options until you have no option left other than finally having to take the plunge.

Also, the information exposure we have today has made us even more aware of the possibilities and choices that we could have ended up with and the potential benefits we could've had if we had chosen an alternate path. But that does put a dent in the overall happiness quotient of the present.

But why is more of the choice a problem while it appears to give us a chance at making better decisions? Probably because it leads to more comparisons and regrets if things don't turn out well as they should have.

And it's because of this that many of us should start resisting the temptations or the race for excess of everything around and switch to voluntary simplicity of thought and life in general, a much simpler way of life or a lifestyle choice that minimises the number of decisions and choices we have to take during the day and also pulls the plug on the pursuit of more of everything except for the priorities, for that matter.

When there are fewer decisions, fewer comparisons, and less chaos, there is more peace and more of life the way you want it.

Comparison corrupts your idea of happiness, and you must realise that everyone's life is messed up in some way or the other. And by merely looking at the highlights of the life of others on social media and the internet, you only have access to a few minutes of their time in their daily lives and not the full picture.

Someone could live in a palatial home, have enough wealth, travel frequently, and have more stuff than they will ever use, but can still be unhappy for various reasons. It could be a messy relationship, some unfulfilled aspiration, or wanting something someone else owns.

The 'What would it have been like if' is something that troubles most of us when we look back, and the past events and decisions consume us. The mind, after that thought, doesn't even consider the things that possibly could've gone wrong with the alternatives available at that time.

Also, if all of your peers are happy in a similar way, i.e. have life conditions comparable yours, you start to assume your state of being as only decent since it's available to everyone else, and you start looking for a better way to feel merrier and better than them.

Are you really not happy or sad, or is it just that feeling of emptiness? Or are you just plain bored and looking for something out of the monotonous life?

Or do you keep wanting something for no reason and feel bad about not being able to get it? It probably is nothing but the mind's natural tendency to be restless when overwhelmed with a lot of information and situations.

The human mind is so fickle that it changes the state of itself in an instant and keeps jumping from one mood to another frequently even with the occurrence of events so redundant that they should not even matter.

Angry because someone disagreed with us in public, anxious because of slow progress, worried about what will happen if we lose our job and concerned because of greying hair. Since the emotions attached to the state of mind are mostly vague at their occurrence, it's impossible to find a pattern for us to find a solution other than to keep the mind at peace and neutral to anything that cannot be controlled.

The mind also gets bored with even the most exciting state of being if it's repeated again. Something that's done again and again ceases to be exciting when it has become a routine.

The first time of anything, be it buying your first car, your first foreign trip, or your first date, happens only for the first time, and nothing can match the adrenaline rush of that. And since every time after that, when you do the same, you know most of what's coming, the pleasant feeling of the unknown starts receding.

Change is the only constant, and in a way, the only way to remain interested in life is to always have something new to look forward to that keeps you motivated and in a positive frame of mind. And while this keeps you busy; it also motivates you to work harder to improve your skills and attributes.

This could even involve small things like learning music, playing a sport, enhancing your fitness, and overall well-being.

If we keep doing the same thing repeatedly, it causes boredom first and then a burnout and sometimes results in us not being able to stand something we liked the most at a time. Even when you exercise in a gym and keep doing the same patterns again and again, or when you have to do the same work at the office for days and months, the monotonous life and systems do get to you after a point of time, and it's even worse when it involves something you didn't like in the first place.

On the flip side, doing the same thing repeatedly is the only way towards being successful in a domain but it's equally important to find that one thing that you are truly passionate about.

Michael J. Fox once said, "My happiness grows in direct proportion to my acceptance and in inverse proportion to my expectations."

The less we expect from people and situations, the more the mind knows how to behave in a neutral way since there are no emotions attached to the expectations of return of investment or the effort from the outcome. And sometimes it feels much better to be involved in or contributing to something without ever expecting anything in return.

The less we expect for ourselves and more towards the outcome of a joint effort, the more we are satisfied with the end result, for it provides us with the immediate closure of all of it at that very moment.

There is no one achievement, landmark, or relationship that can keep you eternally happy, even if you are absolutely comfortable with resting on your laurels. Yes, a state of being content and pursuing gradual progress is possible, in which you are satisfied with what you have at this moment.

And that sometimes is a feasible and calmer position to be in since it's possible to stay in that bracket for a long time and still do things that you like alongside.

Happiness depends on what you find it in, while also knowing that it's not possible to be in a constant ecstatic state of mind. Rather, it is good to always consider having something to look forward to in your life as the normal state of it and prepare to be present in that very moment when it happens and not let it pass by being distracted with the thoughts and worries of the past and the future. It's more about how we engage in things happening in life than always wanting our lives to be a certain way.

If you have survived the Covid pandemic unscathed, if you have never seen a war or famine, a major life-threatening accident or illness, if you have access to all the basics of life, and even if you are even doing just OK with your relationships, physical and mental health, you remain amongst the top 1% happiest population of the world.

It's time you realise it and take it into account when counting your personal happiness index in this chaotic world, a world where a normal life is the new happy state of being.

It's easy to ask you to have a balanced life, but it's a tricky word, for your life isn't completely yours and it's hard to maintain balance while several aspects, people, and situations, sometimes inevitable, are pulling you away from it every day.

It's a notion seldom achieved for a life that asks you to go with the flow and avoiding standing still. What can be asked though is to get your priorities right in accordance with what you want to achieve or the experiences you want to build and learn to try and avoid the worldly noise that comes in the way of it. Decide what deserves your time and energy and avoid the redundant.

It's sometimes foolish to worry about the unknown future and ruin the present, but it's also not wise to not plan for the future when you know that tough times may be ahead since the world is only going to get more chaotic from here on.

Alternatively, chaos and uncertainty of the future remain to be a not-so-simple but an inevitable aspect of life since you have little or absolutely no control over it and can do nothing to change it. And it doesn't always have to be larger than life for you to make the most of your time here and be happy, not in anyone else's terms at least.

In some time, we all would be gone. Our possessions will either have been rendered useless or will belong to someone else. Our positions and legacy that we spent a lifetime to build wouldn't even matter to anyone or, if it even does somewhat, we can't be sure of the narrative of what we did that would be carried forward and the effect it will have.

The coming generations will hardly remember who we are and probably it wouldn't matter to them at all. All in oblivion, in a few decades, everyone and everything will be forgotten eventually. With all of this, does worrying about most of the things that trouble us right now even make an iota of sense?

We don't need to escape the matrix completely, for it may not be even possible with the obligations and responsibilities we are surrounded by, as a part of a family and society. We just need to have a good time and life while in it for a lifetime.

It's not always required to define a purpose that should have a contribution to the world order or match the success and failure definitions of the world around. You could simply be growing a garden or drawing a painting and be happy doing it, or it could simply be spending time with your loved ones or even doing absolutely nothing for that matter, as it's more a matter of choice than having to do it a certain way or as per someone else.

It also remains true that most of us would not be successful to the extent that we all wish for, not live the life we have been made to believe that we deserve. There will still be a lot of things left to do at the end, and we would wish we had more time, but till then all the time we had here would be gone.

Don't be too harsh on yourself because a lot of factors amongst all that govern your life aren't always in your control.

Life doesn't always have to be a make-or-break project or to be considered a waste if something wished for isn't achieved.

It's a wrong belief that something outside of us is the key to eternal happiness, and we must achieve it to stay ecstatic forever. It's all in the mind, and if you don't train your mind to be happy with a simple process, the complexities of this world will ruin your fun.

It's imperative to allow yourself to live a good life while you can by possibly ignoring the redundant noise of the world and not wait for the perfect moment to feel happy or ecstatic, for sometimes we overlook the joys within the simple things of life while the concern for the complex takes over. Don't wait for something to happen to make you happy while your time fades away.

And keep trying for things that you want to do or achieve and find your happy moments within or alongside them so that even if someday life comes a full circle, you would've lived a good one already.

People choose different ways and means of reaching there but in the end, all that's everyone is looking for is to stay happy. Nothing less, nothing more.

On the way, we have to be open and accepting toward emotions like fear, excitement, anxiety, disgust, boredom, anger, and others, since it would be impossible to achieve or become what you aspire to, without experiencing these in the process. It is the presence of all these emotions, in a process that involves overcoming the negative ones to achieve the positive ones, that makes us cherish the happy moments even more.

Being disappointed, heartbroken, sad, and angry about life and situations, and then gathering the will and courage to fight back, regain normalcy, and start again—that's what a fulfilling life is about, and that's what makes the end result even more worth it.

Wouldn't it be great losing track of the time while doing something that you love to? it's only the present and being in it completely that can give you that.

As the Grand Master Oogway says, "Yesterday is history, Tomorrow is a mystery, but today is a gift, that is why it's called The Present.'

***

2

The Random

Is everything destined?
If so, is it possible to predict the future??

Just before the 2021 T20 World Cup semifinal, a leading news channel aired an episode featuring a panel of experts calculating the Indian cricket team's chances. All of them had a similar view in favour of the Indian team, while some even went to the lengths of calling it a 'shat pratishat' (100 percent) one-sided match in which the Indian team will emerge victorious. As per them, all the available data and studies involving the effect of positions and movements of planets and stars on the event suggested so.

At the end, it wasn't even a contest. India lost that match by ten wickets, and not at any one moment while the England team was chasing the target it appeared that there could be a result that's otherwise.

What really happened that day? Was only the data of the players of the Indian team were taken into account, and the same for people involved in the opposing team was not considered? Or did the experts got swayed by their emotions themselves and went ahead with the populist view?

And is it even possible to access and curate all the data on every aspect and factor affecting the outcome of an event?

Even if they thought it was possible and tried to consider all the available data, the actual data required would be far more extensive than what initially meets the eye.

It may not even be possible to correlate all that data to form the odds against or in favour of a certain outcome, considering that not only the playing eleven but a number of other people and factors are also involved in a team's performance on a particular day. The players, the extras on the bench, the team management, selectors all of them have a certain involvement towards the final team in one form or the other.

Is there such a thing as a certain prediction, or should such predictions always be taken with a pinch of salt?

The theory of randomness suggests all events in our lives are a random phenomenon, mostly owing to the fact that it takes a multitude of factors or variable possible outcomes for the occurrence of a certain event, most of which are not in the control of a single entity. Yet, if all the factors are striving towards a single goal, the probability or the odds in favour of the occurrence of an event increases.

Thus, although it's all random, there certainly still are chances where certain aspects or factors affect the probability of a predictable outcome. If not by having a direct but sometimes an indirect involvement in the aspects of the resultant possibles.

Along the similar lines, there are a lot of studies which state that the positions of the stars and the planets have a significant impact on how our life shapes up; the physical features or the lines in our hands can ascertain what the future holds, the architecture of our place of being can help balance the positive and negative energies and thus if managed in a certain way can contribute to or hinder our progress, an insight into the future and the past can be gained picking up some random cards, or a total of some important numbers in your life can indicate the impending random possibilities.'

The mentions in those studies are believed to be able to calculate or inform of the possibility of the occurrence of certain events in our lives or a way to avoid some much before they do actually happen, sometimes with a high degree of certainty claims.

But then, how is it possible that different students of the same science sometimes come to different conclusions even when having access to the same set of data? Or on the flip side, how can all come to a similar conclusion while considering different sets of data and still be wrong about it. If it's related to different interpretations, how to be sure which one of them is to be trusted and followed.

Or is it that the external factors affecting a certain event (also the ever-changing positions of stars and planets in some cases) are dynamic and keep altering, thus resulting in a volatile scenario.

If it was only us living in a secluded scenario, it would've been easier to conclude that some factors can affect your way of being, the future, and all else. But nothing involving you can ever be only because of you and your individual statistics as it always will also involve the dataset of a host of other people and possible outcomes of their actions as well.

HOPE

Let's examine the human tendency to know the future and why we are so inclined towards it.

One way to look at it is that we use all sorts of statistics and mechanisms to support the favourable outcomes we are seeking, which in other words is termed as 'Hope,' an optimistic state of mind in which the subconscious starts finding evidence and situations in support of what we really want to happen.

The basic tenets of human life and relationships are governed by emotions in their various forms, and with all the problems we face in our lives, hope for the solutions to all the problems always exists in the subconscious.

In distressing times, people increasingly turn towards anything that can provide them hope, a possibility towards a better tomorrow in one form or another, which, in turn, helps them get through the day and prevents them from despair.

Sometimes, people intentionally and inherently choose to believe that tomorrow will be better than today, even if the assurance comes from something that actually has no basis, probably as a coping mechanism for the current state of affairs and challenges.

The tendency to base beliefs in favour of the positive probables rather than objective facts, sometimes drives the showcased trust in a lot of studies that claim to predict or ascertain the future.

It may actually work many times, as we have a tendency to make better decisions and put in more effort with a positive frame of mind or when there is a sense of control, which may lead to the positive outcomes we had imagined as a result of it in the first place.

That could precisely be the reason why prediction sciences or studies are gaining popularity, as they claim to provide solutions to the current and the future problems. Since human instinct approves of predictable outcomes and finds comfort within them, we tend to find reassurance in explanations that suggest a clear process leading to the desired result.

When a society or its people are under stress or doubt, they tend to get more inclined towards prediction techniques to find hope for a better future.

It's a good feeling to be hopeful, and it is futile to attempt anything without believing that we could succeed; optimism is, in fact, a good state of mind to live in.

It's hope which doesn't fade away and keeps us optimistic while in trouble, so how can it be a negative sentiment in any situation. Life without hope for the better sounds like a life not worth living at all.

But, like everything else, there is again a thin line between realistic hope and a utopian one. False hope can keep you waiting for things to happen that aren't even probable, pushing you into a biased inaction, hoping that things will get better with time itself.

'Entropy' is the measure of the disorder of the system which explains why life gets more complicated as it goes on, especially with the introduction of more variables in it. It could be anything from relationships to responsibilities or sometimes from simple things like knowing and interacting with more people with time.

If situations leading to it are left unresolved, the disorder will only increase as there would be more variables added to the pile at the same time.

An ordered life could be attained with seclusion and discipline, though there still are outside factors involved to some extent, adding to the disorder. To put things in perspective, we cannot expect everything to remain in order by default, and maintain various aspects of life like relationships, finances, careers, health, and knowledge, it requires continuous efforts, and one cannot rest on past laurels and behaviours and stop the efforts towards the better for it will only invite more chaos into the system.

Imagine being in a state of constant order, and everything remains the same once we leave it at that. It may sound nice, not having to work towards constant betterment once something is executed or achieved but it would stifle creativity, innovation, and growth.

In a similar viewpoint, Murphy's Law says, "Anything that can go wrong will go wrong," which adds to the disorder in most ways possible. Most of us would be able to relate to it owing to the fact that solutions to the problem take a lot of time and effort while the problems, big or small, seem to pop up on their own frequently. The natural inclination of things, when left to themselves and tasks to attain disorder, is the way various aspects of life work.

Without substantial effort, things, relations, career, Health everything can decay within the time cycle of their own, even if left undisturbed.

Similarly, it's the environment that adds value to the order we want to create. You could be a musician living in a society that doesn't want its people to pursue music, or a family that wants you to become a doctor rather than the sportsperson you want to be.

You may have a combination of many unique talents, but being in a supportive environment that provides opportunities and motivation is more valuable to your pursuit than being in one that works against you, creating disorder and requiring substantial extra effort to make situations go in your favour.

The more disorder and randomness in your vicinity, the more random outcomes you will need to go in your favour. Most of the time, you will have to put in extra effort to increase the odds of favourable outcomes.

There are obviously more ways things can go wrong than they can go right. Problems don't always present themselves because the stars are misaligned, or some planets don't have a positive effect on us for any period of time; it may just be the accumulation of disorder or chaotic variables working against us.

There can be more disordered states in life than ordered ones, which is connected to the simple law of probability. Sometimes, it's better to convince yourself that it's almost impossible to solve every situation that life throws at you and be okay with some disorder to find your peace.

We try to find patterns in everything because it informs us of a possible outcome in the future, and due to this, it sometimes gets difficult to absorb the randomness of everything. There are processes and results that are impossible to predict, irrespective of the amounts of historical or current data is available to support it.

The roll of the die will still have a probability of 1/6 for every possible outcome; the flip of a coin will always have a 50–50 chance of landing on either side, irrespective of the history of previous rolls and flips.

Every play is independent of the previous one, and we cannot hope for a certain outcome just because we have had outcomes in our favour or have been having a winning or losing streak in the past.

The same could have been observed in the 2023 Cricket World Cup final, where India played on their home ground against Australia. The Indian team had won ten consecutive matches on their way to the final and looked unbeatable, citing their record-winning streak. But the truth is that irrespective of the previous performance, the chances of one team's win remained at 50-50 since any match remains an independent event.

The Indian team lost ultimately, ending their winning streak throughout the World Cup, but as stated, it obviously could've gone either way anyway with both teams bringing their A game to the finals.

The predictions can make you feel better, but they have nothing to do with the chances of being right or wrong with a definitive accuracy until it's a secluded scenario where all the variables can be known and considered. Most times, it could just be the placebo effect where we generally feel happier living in an optimistic scenario rather than not having anything to look forward to in life.

But this could also mean that the possible outcome declarations can make us make rash and irrational decisions, claiming the already known outcome, and it can, most of the time, be a deterrent in the way of an actual expected one.

What if we are told or know that we are to win that next game of poker? Would the bet size remain the same, or will there be an innate urge to increase the bet size to make more money out of a certain favourable situation?

Similar scenarios keep happening in a financial market trading setup, where when looked through the window of hope, we are always bound to make bad decisions and actions and regret it later after losing a fortune, only to learn that nothing is certain and a 100% and that the bets must remain sane in order of the calculated risk profile, even when the odds are favouring you, for they are just the odds, and there the downside has to be defined to avoid unlimited risk.

There can also be correlated outcomes in which the occurrence of one depends a lot on the result of the other.

Consider a cricket match where the team batting first may have a real advantage based on the weather or pitch conditions. The result of the coin toss event may have a major impact on the other big outcome, i.e., the result of the match.

The same toss in which the probability of either outcome remains to be 50-50. A classic case one outcome leads to odds being in favour of another.

In sports, the better team doesn't always win. There are instances when a less competitive team has their way against a giant when most events during the match go in their favor and some do not favour the favourites.

Let us consider a relatively independent event: the coin toss.

Researchers have even tried to build robots that can throw coins at the same speed and force in a controlled atmosphere, resulting in the same height achieved in every flip and with the same momentum and angle of flight. The more we can control the affecting factors, the result can be assessed with a lot more accuracy, but not always, as the dynamic factors will still keep changing while the event execution is at it.

This happens to be the case with every scenario; the fewer the number of variables, the more it's possible to control or predict the outcome of a situation, and thus, the chances in favour of an outcome can be created.

If we ignore the above experiments, in the real world, such is only possible through repeating the same process, again and again, to understand and ultimately be in control of all or most of the variables that you can control and execute your actions according to them. If the description wasn't this complex, the process could simply be called 'Practice' or preparation for the impending or upcoming.

And if there are still certain factors left, even after creating a controlled atmosphere or a practised or prepared-for situation that will affect the resultant, it still increases the chances of us being on the winning side. It creates or adds to the odds in our favour, even though the count of the uncontrollable factors is the same, the probability of them falling in our favour is now much more. In other words, since the odds are in our favour because of the 'practised' situation, we can leave what's left to what we can call luck or the alignment of unpredictable circumstances or outcomes that lead to a favourable outcome.

Take up any sport and see the legends who have practised their art day in and day out all their lives, working on their fitness and temperament. It will still hit you that though they are almost perfect at their art, they still keep failing, though probably a smaller number of times than they win or perform well. The net sum of which also shows up in their career records but still not always in terms of more wins than losses or more successes than failures but mostly about their graph being more than the historical averages of previously successful people in that very sport.

That is, in fact, all we can do—try to improve upon the number of factors in our reach with practice and preparation. Then it would be pertinent to hope and depend on the stars to favour us to align the uncontrollable in our favour, creating the magical world that we attribute a lot to—*The 'Luck'*.

While we consider the term "absolutely random," its nature is not. Good luck outcomes are still aligned to be among the only possible results, and with some random interference, results can still go either way.

If you didn't make the move, there would be no event for the stars to turn in your favour. If you don't persevere, you don't give enough time and events to the stars to tilt in your favour.

From the perspective of probability theory, Dr. Strange in the movie 'The Avengers: End Game' informed Iron Man that there were 14 million possible outcomes of the war they were entering, and each of those outcomes was equally likely to occur. And there was only one event out of those 14 million in which they could win the war. In all others, the Avengers would end up losing.

That one favourable outcome required a lot of events to happen and not happen a certain way if the Avengers were to attain victory over Thanos and his army.

That certain intricate path for an event to take place requires a whole lot of factors to work in a certain way and also not to happen in a certain way for it to result in its final form.

There are some instances where people calculate the ratio of luck in a particular success story or happening. If you could assess it with all that's said above, it's still impossible to calculate it precisely. It could only be the dumb luck or complete fortune which happens all by chance, and you have zero percent effort or involvement in the result.

Like finding an opportunity lost by someone else, a wild guess gone right in a multiple-choice test, or being born at a certain time, place, and identity, a severe illness wiping out your wealth and time. But all of these still cannot be called completely independent events.

Warren Buffett has also been an endorser of the involvement of luck in all aspects of life. In his annual letter, he mentioned being thankful for being born in the US at a particular time, which he insists played a huge role in his success.

Meeting certain people in his life, finding the right connections, the resources, and circumstances are all he credits for where he is right now rightly so, because all of these are just random occurrences that needed just the right timing to happen and work out well.

But when it's not just the dumb luck involved, every individual has instances of good and bad luck. It's only when it aligns with the preparation or the karma that the chances of a favourable outcome will increase. It's also true that a random stroke of bad luck can negatively impact the result, irrespective of the amount of work that has gone in.

It would be just to say if 90% of the factors are controllable, and still 10% are random, then also the probability of the event will remain in ratio to the number of possible outcomes.

In cricket, an exceptional batsman can get out first ball with a great piece of bowling or fielding. That same person can go on to make a century if a catch is dropped or the bowlers are not able to take his wicket that day.

Yes, 'the day,' that's what they mean when they say it. It wasn't his day when they couldn't perform well, indirectly attributing it to luck since the player is already amazing at his art.

And when it's all done and dusted, we can be as thankful to our own preparation or karma as well as to the random favourable or the luck, though in variable percentages.

And if the above is true, is there anything you cannot predict the chances of occurring to some extent, if you knew and calculated all the factors and patterns related to it? Because even the most random events have a tendency to produce patterns, and sometimes, it's only as random as it's assumed to be.

Sometimes, the patterns and calculations work, and sometimes, they don't. Accidents happen to good people as well as the bad ones. Good things sometimes happen to the undeserving. But since life is a mixed bag for all of us, we tend to correlate the events with what has been predicted or believed.

Some say, if we are in trouble, it's obviously some sin from the past that has resulted in this or the destiny that cannot be changed. But when is it that we aren't in trouble, big or small, one aspect or the other? Isn't it always the scenario?

And it's sometimes easier to call things random and destined and not practise towards the controllable factors of an outcome and play the ignorance or procrastinate towards failure. It's time we understand that every single result we achieve in life will have a combination of karma, preparation, and the chances of the variables to favour you in the form of luck, destined or random.

And when they say fortune favours the brave, it's because of the fact that they are brave enough to keep trying for the favourable outcome since no action and all hope will only place the entire relevance of achieving something on the uncontrollable scenarios and the stars.

Contrary to what we believe and are told, and what the experts at these subjects will tell you, the purpose of these studies and science is to be a guiding force and not to certainly predict an event.

This is the very assumption people make, thinking that any calculation can predict a certain event in the future. These sciences will always seem to work to some extent, but the assumption and claims of certainty are where the whole problem lies.

At certain times, a common description may seem to apply to everyone at once. Most people can relate to it and believe that it's actually a lot about them and what's happening in their lives, regardless of it being a generic version of relatable possibilities for a whole lot. Online personality tests, fortune-telling, and horoscopes published in newspapers use this effect to actually seem useful and applicable in most scenarios.

But what if we start to believe that whatever is written has to happen anyhow and give up on what we really want to do?

Sometimes we plan our lives and future as if everything will remain perfect and just about everything will start to fall in place. But, in reality, we are just doing a futile exercise when we try to exert control over the uncontrollable. Sometimes, it's also depressing to feel that it doesn't matter how much effort you make at something; the results are never in line with what you had planned for, for no reason.

The absolute fact remains that there is only one variable amongst all others that you can control, and that's the work and the effort that we put in, the choices and the habits that we develop.

For all else that's not under our control, to go in our direction, we can only wait for that stroke of luck, divine intervention or the planetary forces to work in our favour.

Also, you don't really have to know what's going to happen tomorrow because it will happen irrespective of you being aware of it or not. Yes, you can argue that you will be able to avoid certain scenarios in life if you are already aware of the possibilities, but then again, whatever you assume or know based on your studies isn't always 100% certain.

"It's nearly impossible to align the potential outcomes from all the studies to your advantage. Each study and science carries variable probabilities for any event and may sometimes point to entirely different conclusions."

The beauty of life remains in not knowing and not assuming what lies ahead, as it gives us the opportunity to strive and hustle towards making things better than they are now, towards how we want to shape our lives. Our minds need not be cluttered with the pre-decided outcome informed based on not what we want to put in the effort for, but the positions of the stars and the planets, and to add to it, the time and place of birth on which we absolutely had no control.

You can choose to believe in the predictions and the calculations, and your trust in it may also have a certain valid argument attached to it, but then again, it may not be true for everyone else or for all situations.

If there is a destined path or a destination for you that has already been decided, it will also have to be supported by your actions and choices, however random they are.

You still need to buy a ticket to win that lottery, right? Moreover, that ticket has to be left on the shelf for you to buy and not already have been bought by someone else.

Embracing the random while trying to make everything better with our choices and actions, striving and fighting for it, sometimes being sad and angry, tearful and ecstatic… not knowing what tomorrow holds for us except for the beautiful possibilities, deciding not to predict it, and just taking it as it comes and live to fight another day, even if today wasn't in favour. That's what makes us human, right?

✳ ✳ ✳

3
Chaos

Right now, there is just too much of it.
And it's messing up our minds.

What does it look like in our everyday lives?

For the great bunch of us, it's a whole lot of people and situations to deal with on a daily basis, and also the expectations and perspectives in relationships and the random emotions that come with it, the act as per the rights and wrongs of society, things not going the way you want them to, and the all-day inflow of mostly redundant information.

It sometimes gets impossible to make a choice or a decision with all of this, and even when it's made, it makes us think if we could've made a better one since whatever we go ahead with ends up upsetting certain aspects of our lives and some people present in it.

Though chaos is the law of nature, less of it always helps to stay sane and stay focused on what we want to do or achieve.

But many don't have the privilege to wake up every day and do only what excite them or follow the process towards their goal. Sometimes you have to do things that you would rather not, for the sake of commitments and obligations.

Some people like chaos, and it brings out the best of them, while some want to live in order and peace and find it absolutely distracting to deal with anything random. Many times, there is too much happening in life at once that you get overwhelmed with it and just want to run away or take a break from the chaos.

Chaos in the initial stages of life is an essential lesson, and some people get bored by the order and use chaos as motivation for growth, and it's imperative to learn to handle chaos than to completely ignore the aspects causing it. Also, because we need to go through infinite possibilities and experiments before one can choose the final path.

Life is chaotic in its very nature, and paying heed to the surroundings only amplifies the chaos, and though you cannot control what is happening in the world, you sure can choose to stay away from some of it.

But there is a difference between the chaos and the randomness of life; while the latter is inevitable, the involvement in chaos can be controlled to some extent with conscious effort and the knowledge of what we want to devote our time to and what to say yes and no to for the better.

The thing with chaos is that if allowed to take over the process, it multiplies, with a little more of every single element adding to the final result. And if there has been much of it since the beginning, the resultant of the effort may end up far from what we wanted it to.

But after a certain time, it gets too much to deal with, especially when it starts to have a negative impact on your mental, emotional, and physical well-being.

That's exactly why 'less is the new more,' and it sometimes takes us half a lifetime to understand that.

"A few friends are more than enough to share the good times; only a few things of all you own are useful, and only a few tasks deserve most of your time and

undivided attention, and most of everything else is just unwanted clutter or the noise of the world."

Living with less means fewer choices and decisions to make, which ultimately helps avoid the paradox of choice that we face with the increasing number of trivial decisions we have to make in our daily lives.

Minimalism.

It's intentionally living with things that we really need, removing the clutter and, along with it, the distractions and choices. In a race for a fast life, being a minimalist essentially slows you down and only lets you deal with things that you really want to.

Though less doesn't really need to be close to none, and your way of doing it depends on your view of necessity, in any way, it will result in more time for you and less stress of choices and decisions.

While 'minimalism' is all about only adding or buying that adds value to your life, mental minimalism is about changing your mindset to accommodate less clutter and more meaning. *Focus on more of what's important than what's not by eliminating the distractions. Being mindful and in the moment and not allowing the clutter and chaos in the mind to take away the precious, dear moments of life.*

The mind is a complex machine, and you have to be mindful of what you feed it, for what goes in isn't always defined as useful or redundant and adds to the chaos anyway, even if you choose to ignore it.

Too many thoughts are a result of too much information and impending decisions and choices.

The only way is to get rid of the unwanted chaos and stop your mind from getting overwhelmed. It's also a deterrent when you always want to believe that something important is yet to be known before moving ahead. And it is this very thought with which you start providing reasons to your mind for procrastination.

In today's times, it becomes the most sought-after ability to reduce the clutter in the mind at will, to be able to think straight and focus for long on the task at hand and not be distracted again and again by the impulses to do something else and be somewhere else.

What's mentioned here is more of mindful minimalism than the real meaning of it, being conscious about what we need or buy, the tasks we say yes to, being intentional with what to let the mind absorb and reject, what to pay heed to and what not to, so that at the end of the day you can get back to your life without the baggage and the clutter of the world.

But the source of it isn't only about what goes in the mind but what's around us as well. It's mainly the lifestyle, that of the excesses that we live currently where we have a multitude of choices for every decision we have to make during the day.

And the minimalism that's being discussed can be applied to everything from belongings, relationships, commitments, and even to information consumed. Only that till now, we used to realise the importance of it at the later stages of life.

But as chaotic as the world has started to become, it's imperative that we understand and start to follow it from the word go.

It's easy to get overwhelmed with a lot of things in this world where you want to be a part of anything and everything, buy things on impulse that we never use, search happiness in the clutter of social life and contacts, and seek chaos just for the fear of missing out (FOMO).

But focus only works when you are doing one thing at a time and not thinking about a lot of others while doing it, not being caught in the past and the future, not in the maze of thoughts but just being in the present and that very moment.

It's a difficult skill to master and execute, but once you manage to do it, it will be easier to avoid the usual distractions and be mindful of the task at hand.

However, is it even possible that while consuming all the information and chaos that comes our way, we can still maintain a state of minimal thoughts at a certain moment? And the information received is used and recalled only when it's needed or else lies in the subconscious. If it were possible, it could be the most attainable way of staying sane amidst the chaos when not being able to reject or stay away from it.

And while it's considered that most people have trouble with their attention span these days, it may not exactly be the problem. Like everything else, the reason and the 'why' of the task are of utmost importance since that reason will only give you the motivation to stick to and focus on that single task and avoid all distractions.

If you don't know exactly why you are doing it, it's a vicious infinite loop of getting into redundant things and tasks.

That 'why' or the accountability factor of it could be towards a deadline or a commitment towards some event or person or sometimes towards something you are already motivated for.

"Find a reason good enough or an accountability strong enough, and you will find your focus, discipline and the patience to do it."

Opportunity Cost

What if you had an invite from four different events at the same time, and what if the one you didn't go to turns out to be the better one… or what useful you could've done with all that time you wasted on social media.

If you were allowed to buy only one of the two potentially bullish stocks in the market, and the one you didn't buy turned out to give much better results in the long-term than the one you actually did? What feelings would that lead to?

And sometimes, even though you want to go ahead with all the choices available because either you like them equally or each has some aspect better than the other it may not be possible for some reason.

When faced with the choice of managing or using only one thing at a time, how do we decide?

Like buying a phone, the decision in which we often have to decide between the iOS and Android devices, or when buying a car, which makes us choose between different models of various companies. It's a difficult choice, but it can only be one that we can go ahead with.

It is a fundamental concept of economics which refers to the potential advantage lost from an alternate choice or a missed opportunity. In other words, it's a benefit you miss out on when you choose or make one decision over another.

It could range from very small to big decisions of life, from buying that T-shirt or a car to choosing one career option over another. And though some of these costs are negligible, others could leave us dissatisfied for life when compared with what might have happened if we had chosen alternative options.

Sometimes, we have a lot of choices for what we want to do with our time and resources, and though we always try to make informed decisions and choose the best available one as per our knowledge and inclinations, all informed decisions don't turn out to be the best resulting ones at the end.

Also, there is an opportunity cost attached to everything. The cost of choosing one alternative over the other, be it your finances, time or other life choices, and living with the consequences of having made that decision and sometimes with the regret of something you could've said yes or no to.

Every option you choose leaves another option on your table unattended, and sometimes you have to say no to a lot of good things in life for even better ones or to be more productive at things you have already said yes to and committed to.

And it's obvious that we cannot say yes to everything that comes our way whatever the opportunity cost attached. Saying no to tasks and commitments that aren't relevant to you remains one of the most significant productivity hack of all time.

Moreover, the opportunity cost of your time increases as you become more successful. That's why it becomes more important to be able to say no or learn to refuse to be a part of something that we don't want to be involved in or anything that doesn't add any value to our cause. And it still remains the number one way to reclaim your time, to save you from a lot of stress in the future.

But why do they call it an art? Probably because It's difficult to say no sometimes because it's difficult to hear one as well.

But if it's resulting in putting other people's needs and requirements above your own and is affecting your focus and purpose, it must stop.

We agree to a lot of things because we sometimes feel that it would be disrespectful to say no to something that's asked as a request, and we don't want to come across as rude or unhelpful.

And there are moments it just becomes impossible to disagree or refuse. There may be people associated you don't want to let down or some relationships at stake, or a concern of discomfort we may be causing.

If your inclination and intention is clear enough, being sorry immediately may be far better than taking time to think over it and refusing later. For it creates hope and expectations of a yes. We can choose to feel the pain of that 'no' now or feel the pain of yes for long.

If you are useful, people will ask for favours, sometimes monetary and some in terms of your presence, time, and energy. And it's obvious that we cannot get into any number of situations and handle them well. There is a limit to what we can pay attention to, and it may be counterproductive to always blurt out yes when it's a no from within and suffer for days and weeks because of it.

Whenever we do that, we tend to make ourselves vulnerable to getting overwhelmed with too many tasks at once or with something that makes us wish for a long time that we shouldn't have agreed to it.

As James Clear said in his book 'No is a decision while yes is a responsibility'. And when we say no, we are in a better place to agree to something more useful and allot our time to it and be more productive towards our cause. Or even do nothing with it than waste it on irrelevant commitments.

Because when we are saying yes to something, it takes away our capacity to say yes to anything else for the duration. Once we learn to say no, we will indirectly start to focus on what we've said yes to mindfully.

It doesn't always apply only to the external requests but also to the internal impulses of the mind. Saying no to distractions and yes to discipline and minimalism. Saying no to the chaos and yes to the peace of mind. A yes to the good habits and no to the bad ones, the process that contributes a lot in turning us into who we want to become.

Habits

Bad habits are much easier to form, for they mostly rely on the comfort or the instant gratification impulses and do not take into account the long-term scenario of the good and bad aspects of it. While the good ones may be boring and appear pointless at the start, the bad ones are instantly satisfying, and provide that dopamine or endorphin boost, and make us feel better with it in those immediate moments.

For instance, staying up late gives way to comforting use of social media, eating junk food has a reward for the taste buds. Compare it with the supposedly good ones that add value to life. Reading often is slow and boring, regular exercises need effort and take much longer for the results to be visible.

We are inclined to fall for the swift and be wary of the slow in these times, moreover when a whole lot of choices keep spoiling our thought process to choose the easiest way out in the present. But there are certain things that only the process and the practice can make possible. It is probably the discomfort of now versus the better for the long-term situation that we need to choose between.

The goal of the process is to excel, succeed in the game, and perform at your best. The cycle of improvement can persist even after achieving the desired result.

And for that, it's imperative to establish an accountability system that attaches every success and failure to something or someone that you fear or value much more than the habit that you cannot get rid of. That is something for you to figure out before you begin, or else you would just be wasting your time trying the impossible.

It would also always be better to fill the void created by leaving one habit and to fill it with another one. With bad habits, it's an infinite loop since the subconscious also wants to repeat them if there is time available and no accountability systems are placed for their avoidance.

And it's only when you have achieved that state of reduced chaos in the mind and in life, have figured out your accountability systems, and have become better at managing your time and commitments, it's only then that we can start to move ahead with life-forming habits and discipline.

For if we attempt to do that without exercising self-control over emotions and time allocation, it would be a futile exercise since distractions will keep coming in, and the consistent execution of the process will be affected.

It would be like starting to exercise and not continuing with it, beginning to read a book but leaving it halfway, practising that art but not being mindful while doing it. It doesn't get us anywhere, more often than not we find ourselves at the starting point again and again.

If you wish to harness the power of tiny gains and develop the subconscious love of the process towards what you want to be and achieve, it must take the form of a consistent practice and habit. The small changes in daily life can have a compounding effect on your mindset and growth patterns.

But it's not only about making way for the new; it's also about getting rid of the old. How do you break bad habits or build good ones for that matter?

The immediate step would probably be to find the 'why' of it, the reason strong enough to be able to reject something that you have been doing for long and move on to the new ways of life and then the motivation and accountability setup to help you begin with it.

But what if breaking the habit requires internal strength and will power that we don't always have? It's true that we can't always rely on ourselves for accountability, as impulses often take over and lead us to give in and results in us not being able to break the vicious loop we wanted to get rid of. And it's in such cases that the external sources of accountability can prove to be very useful.

But why are we unable to manage the prolonged level of self-control, discipline, and order that others can? Sometimes it's even difficult to begin with even the smaller tasks, such as organizing a clean office desk, tidying a room, reducing clutter and seeking more clarity in thoughts and beliefs, let alone tackling the bigger ones that have a substantial effect on how our life shapes up.

Many claim to be able to do that, but is it really possible for everyone??

The productivity coaches and theorists even claim to be able to teach the process and help execute it. The perfect schedule and the perfect lifestyle to suit your ambition and goals, and the mindset that helps you get through the difficult times.

But can all of this be taught or is it always a self-learned skill? Since most of what this involves has something to do with the people and chaos around us and how we manage to handle it,

For many of us, the idea of having total control is often an illusion, and the belief in constant 24/7 discipline and productivity is a myth. And even if it were possible for a few who live in a secluded scenario, it's not a realistic or desirable solution for most of us. For it may end up with you hating the exact same thing that you signed up for and have always wanted to do and achieve for years. The very process that once motivated you can lead to burnout and a sense of emptiness over time.

That is exactly why people sometimes feel a lot better after giving up something they have worked their entire lives for.

It's time we give it our 100% and let go of the productivity guilt, a feeling of sadness when we believe that we aren't working that hard, not being productive enough or wasting our time not doing things that could have helped our life and careers which often has us thinking if we aren't good enough for not being able to succeed however hard we try.

It's not about being productive every minute of the day or being devoid of chaos forever and only doing things that are in line with the ultimate goal and the process. Being focused on the task at hand is often more than enough.

Yes, it's a race most of the times but sometimes we are running a lot of them at a single instant, willing or not. And we really don't need to win them all, just navigating through the ones that matter less would just be fine.

There is this beautiful quote by a famous person that says:

"The more you know who you are and what you exactly want, the less you let things upset you."

There is nothing wrong with not pursuing that goal all day long, not being productive every minute of the day, not having that room and office always managed and uncluttered,

No one can be 100% okay all the time, and it's okay to not be okay on some days.

It's also completely okay to not always be disciplined, to not be in the right frame of mind, and taking some time off the routine.

Most of the life situations require us to press the reset button once in a while, unlearn what has been learned, forget and forgive, reject the unwanted emotions and unsee certain situations.

Because once you have given a thought to all that's under your control, you must also acknowledge the presence of a lot of certain factors that you cannot influence.

You may not be lazy, you may not lack focus or patience, but it may be just about finding the right thing or the reason to start working on something, to stick to it and to commit to the process that leads to that end result that you desire.

And if you manage to figure that out, you will have your willpower, patience and your focus back. And if the accountability systems are setup right, it's even possible to match the level of discipline that you were always looking for.

Life cannot be all chaos or all discipline. Too much chaos invites a lot of stress and too much regulation of emotions can leave you exhausted and burnt out.

The net chaos in the world is the result of chaos created by individuals like us, and if you wish to change the chaotic world and surroundings for the better, it would be good way to start if you stop contributing to it.

Order and chaos are the extremes of each other, and it's upon you on which side of life you are planning to move towards, or just stay in the middle for sometimes till you figure out what you like more.

We don't have to follow the crowd or be present everywhere. It's not necessary to always voice our opinions or respond to everyone we disagree with.

Sometimes it's the words that create more problems than actions and using them sparingly and wisely could be your contribution towards less chaos and more order.

4

Money

What's more important than money?
A lot of things if you only ask people who already have
enough of it.
For those who don't, nothing even comes close.

Some would say it's health, relationships and peace that's more important, but it's often the loss or absence of money that reveals its paramount importance and makes us realise that there is nothing more important. If you think otherwise, look around clearly or try living a month without it, and you will quickly see how health, relationships and peace deteriorate without financial resources and realise that it was only the presence of it that had held together the various aspects of our lives.

For anything else to be important enough for anyone and have the time and resources to pursue it, one must have a certain amount of money, at least for the basics to be taken care of.

It's only when you have a good amount of money that the psychology of money comes into play which involves of what you think about it, managing and retaining it, and making more of it while using some of what you already have.

What is also true is that different experiences and beginnings with money, the source and effort involved, make us believe different things about it and value it differently.

While at early stages of life, we only receive it to spend it without realising the effort that has gone into making it. Later, when we actually make it and then have to spend it, it's the process that makes us wiser about the value of it. Also, the surroundings have an effect on our overall perception of it, and value for money or VFM may mean different things to different people.

A whole lot of people will link success to money, and those who do not are probably delusional or already have more than enough of it. Success without money is what very few people will choose if given an option to begin with. They say it's the root of all evil, but the lure of the lucre is indomitable.

It's a proven fact that society at large will judge your stature and success based on the amount of money you have made or can generate for the associates.

You may have a heart of gold, but you cannot go and keep proving it to anyone. Society believes what it can see in an instant, and to prove your success, obviously, it demands to view the whereabouts of your success in the form of wealth. And even if you disregard the society's definition of success and are content with your own, money will still play an important part in enabling you to maintain that belief.

But there is more to money than meets the eye. And you get to see and learn a lot more lessons and reality of the world when you have less or none of it.

It's also important to accept that not everyone has to work as hard as others to make the same amount of money, or sometimes even more. It's also the starting point in life which decides, to a certain extent, all else being equal, how much money you will be able to make over your lifetime.

Though there will be instances when someone who had a lot of it lost most of it during the course of life, and someone who didn't have any in the first place ended up having a lot of it.

That's where the art of making and managing money, the education and experience of doing it and handling the emotions related to it is of utmost importance. Keeping it becomes just as important as, if not more important than, making it. And spending some of the money on learning more about keeping and investing it does no harm at all.

Financial independence is a state when you have enough income via active and passive sources to be able to pay for your living expenses and lifestyle without having to depend on someone else and to be able to make your own independent financial decisions.

We see most elders teach you to start working and save money at an early age for the bad times and save a ratio of what you earn for the times when the tide isn't in your favour, and when you may not be earning that much.

There is nothing wrong with that, though the learnings can be modified a bit to suit the current times, especially if you wish to make progress or to learn the nuances of different sectors to find out if you can identify with some and wish to make an alternate career or a side hustle out of it.

Because if you do not explore, you would not know, and asking to save everything and not spending on the possibilities and learnings can be a lethal piece of advice at this time.

Yes, it's important to save, but equally important to spend a portion of it wisely at a prime age on things and experiences which may help you explore and learn more. It could also help start that alternate career that may fetch you more money than the current one.

The acquisition of knowledge at the right time is equally necessary to find a proper vocation which can fulfil your monetary needs moving forward and provide you with work satisfaction in life. Which, if you ultimately succeed, may end up paying you the worth of the amount saved in all those years in just a short interval of time.

In schools and colleges, we study subjects and lessons which will ultimately help us find a good job or start that business, the motive of which is to earn money and then use it to live a good life. But nowhere do they teach us the most important thing about money — how to manage that money once we start earning it. Personal finance and money management are the most neglected subjects in conventional education formats, even when it's evident that having basic personal finance knowledge is the most important skill we can ever learn to be in control of the monetary aspects of life.

The basic level of understanding of budgets, saving, investments, returns, and debts is as important as earning money. And lack of financial knowledge and its applications has painful consequences. It's high time we include personal finance and money management lessons in our education system since the very start and empower our young to make better decisions.

No one is too young to know about finances and the value of money. If the young can identify the purchasing power of money, they are ready to learn to start spending it wisely, saving, and investing it as well.

It forms the basic foundation of our lives, and learning about it early will only help us make wiser decisions. The current system teaches a lot of things and subjects which we ultimately would not be using during our lifetimes, and we have had to only learn them for the sake of getting good grades in the class.

The majority of parents would want schools and colleges to teach their children about it since they want their kids to understand the value of money and how much hard work it takes to make and manage it.

Since money also remains the major cause of stress in young and adults alike, and everyone at some point of time in their lives has felt financial pain, poorly managed finances can result in destroying other aspects of life such as relationships and health as well. When something has this much of an impact on our lives and still is not included in the learning system, it is weird at best. The youth of today have a different view of finance, and while they want to spend all they earn and have a good time while they can, it makes it all the more important to teach them the importance of starting to invest early.

It's also about controlling impulsive decisions when spending a substantial amount on redundant purchases and asking yourself if it's really needed and useful to you or if you just want to have something because someone else has it. That money, which you could save on something you actually do not need, could well go into an investment in yourself, some memorable experiences, or in an account that will fetch you some positive returns rather than get you a depreciating asset that will only make you happy for a limited amount of time.

Of course, buying good things in life is necessary for a comfortable life and to keep up with your living standard, but conscious consumerism stops you from wasting your hard-earned money on the unwanted and use it elsewhere for a more fruitful outcome.

It's also important to eliminate or reduce debt in your life or bring it to a comfort level of controlled and calculated proportions to avoid unnecessary stress in life. Though manageable debt and stress are sometimes good as they push you to work harder, opting for a huge proportion of it for buying a big house or an emotional asset that will have you commit a major portion of your future income for the payments for the next 20-30 years is something most learned would not advocate.

Sometimes, it's necessary to raise debt for a business venture or expand the current one as we expect to pay it back from the profits we will make from it. It gives an opportunity to those who do not have access to such amounts of money and are willing to work hard to do better in life, but efforts should be made to keep it under check because piling up substantial amounts of debt sooner or later will result in situations difficult to handle, accompanied by a lot of stress and heartburn.

And like everything else, the debt also has an opportunity cost attached to it. It affects your current lifestyle, any other possible investments, and some calculated risks that could have resulted in better returns sans the financial stress. Also, consider the scenario where something goes wrong with your finances or occupation, and you are still required to pay up the monthly instalments.

Yes, there are emotional reasons for purchasing something as important as a house, and it is a dream of a lifetime for many and a reward like no other, but then it's a personal choice for one to make if you are ready to commit your whole life to it and should not be regretful if at the end of all of this, it doesn't seem to be worth it at all for you obviously will have to cut corners and make other sacrifices financially if you want to make it work.

Investments are as important as earning money, and it's time to teach the understanding of the various aspects and basic instruments related to it to the young. Also, the importance of keeping it simple and not getting overwhelmed by the number of instruments available and complex jargon being thrown around.

Age plays an important role in deciding the asset class you can invest your money in as young investors have fewer responsibilities and can take a bit more risk compared to the older ones.

Stock Markets

The stock market could be the all-reward machine if someone can figure out a way to harness the data to calculate the possible outcome even with a 50-60% probability. Even with that kind of mediocre-looking accuracy, anyone can earn bucketloads of money.

Investing in stock markets is an option for those willing to take more risks for higher returns, but it requires serious hard work and discipline to fetch continuous and compounded returns out of it. It's akin to playing with fire for the uninformed, and sometimes, people have also ended up losing all their savings. Very few have been able to keep up with the volatility and uncertainty of it, despite devoting a lot of their time and attention to it.

A lot of things are told to us on social media by money experts and influencers that may not be entirely true or even applicable to us. What remains true is that making money by trading futures in stock markets, is a zero-sum game, and not everyone can make it at once; it can only change hands. There have to be losers for there to be winners, and one person's game typically corresponds to another person's loss. There has to always be a debit for every credit for a constant amount of money in the system. Anyone that tells you otherwise, that everyone can make money at once without anyone losing it, is only making you believe it to profit from it in one way or the other.

Moreover, there may not even be a right or wrong way for you for someone else to tell you that, and it's you who has to decide the ratio and proportion of risk you want to take for the returns you are looking at, the theories you want to believe in and execute in your journey of learning about markets and making more money out of it.

Most of the so-called stock market experts give money-making ideas on social media, claiming huge and seemingly impossible returns on their trading and investment accounts and instruments, mostly to make money out of giving advice or to make you believe that they can teach you how to do the same as well.

But if they actually knew how to make a substantial amount of money with those ideas, they wouldn't be selling them like this and would be using them first-hand to make money for themselves. But obviously, they chose the former as the safer way because they know they can just provide ideas and not execute them for gains. There are some who make money both ways, by providing genuine advice and also by trading and investing in stocks and making sustainable returns, but not all who advise you are making money from their own execution of it; if they do, they will rather not reveal their methods of doing it.

It's not impossible to make money out of the stock market, but there has to be a system to the madness, for it's impossible for a return percentage beyond a certain point to be sustainable for long.

About stock markets, if one has ever monitored them closely enough, though considered high risk, they give us the most important lessons about money and life at once. What sets it apart from other investing and trading instruments is the constantly fluctuating value and rapid pace of change at every moment. Unlike other instruments, which don't manipulate your impulses and emotions as intensely, the price and value movements here are much more rapid and instantaneous. A stock could be priced high one day and destroyed the very next day, depending on the underlying conditions and scenarios.

Whenever we take a trade in the stock markets, it has a stop-loss point (the maximum loss we are willing to take on a certain trading position for a potential profit and the point where we would exit the trade in loss if it reaches there first), plan of position sizing (number of shares or the amount we are willing to invest at that price point), and a target price (a price where we expect the price to reach a certain level above the buy price where we will book the profits of our trade).

The target price set is advisable to be multiple times the stop-loss points, since anything can go wrong, and the profit once made should be able to absorb the losses of a few trades so as to make sense even if the ratio of success is less.

It requires us to set up the trade at a certain time and have patience until either the profit targets are met, or the stop-loss points are hit. Also, if the pricing is range-bound or doesn't touch either of the stipulated levels, it's important to know how much time we are willing to devote to the trade setup, as not all setups can be carried forward another day.

And even when it's possible to carry forward to the next day, still you must be aware of the plan and price levels you need to follow, as carrying forward the positions the next day increases the risk and the amount of uncertainty associated with the trade.

Here are some aspects and life lessons that can be taken from it.

1) **Having a plan and sticking to it**: When you are set to execute the triggers or the buy and sell orders, it's always beneficial to have a plan beforehand. All the details of it, in fact, the point of entrance or involvement, the time period allotted to it, the exit routes if things may go wrong, and the target allotted to it if things go right as per the plan.

   And while it tells you that planning is important, what's difficult but of utmost importance is to also stick to the plan and not give in to the emotional impulses that the frequent movements and chaos create. It doesn't always turn out to be exactly as per the plan, but sticking to it and playing by the rules somewhat allows us to respond to the situations appropriately and not be affected by the emotions attached to it.

Impulsive decisions amidst the chaos can prove to be destructive for the business as well as life situations.

2) **The Risk Reward Ratio**: For every position or decision in life, there is always a risk associated with every reward we are after, sometimes in the form of a big opportunity cost as well. Thus, it makes it important to assess the ratio of what we can lose in the pursuit of what we want to gain. Some risks are always good to take, but the reward has to be multiple times it or substantial enough for it to make sense.

That also includes the probability of us going wrong more than once continuously for various reasons beyond our control. Substantial rewards, in comparison to the risk involved, manage that aspect by providing a cushion for a string of losses or failures. Even if we keep having a decent number of wins compared to losses, it's still profitable and sensible in the long run, in the financial markets and in life.

You just need a few big wins in business and in life, and the number of small losses or failures won't even matter.

3) **Compounding and Patience**: Like everything else, investing needs a lot of work—assessing

different instruments, companies, finding value in the current price, and then devising a plan to execute it in a particular manner.

And when the work is done, the plan needs us to give it time to grow into something that it has the potential to. Compounding of money is a magical process, just like the compounding of habits in life. When stacked over time, the effect of positive habits can compound to bring about some amazing changes and results.

If we can give the process sufficient time and stick to the discipline, the results, though not visible at first, can be enormous in the later cycles of it.

What begins as a small win or potential can grow and compound into something much greater over time, both in terms of money and life, if you have the patience to stick to it.

4) **All asset classes aren't always bullish:**

There was a time when the price of Reliance Industries Stock fluctuated in a range for 10 years. The same has happened with gold, and despite being considered the most precious metal and a global currency, there was a time when its price fell to half of what it was at its peak.

But like everything else in life," *the current price or state of anything or anyone isn't always equal to the value it holds and the potential it promises.*"

And it may take some time for things and results to happen, but anyone can, in spite of their current state of being, with effort and discipline, do justice to the true potential they hold.

5) **It's impossible to time the markets**: Exactly like it's impossible to predict with certainty how life will shape up.

   You just have to accept that there are things that we cannot control and stick to working towards what we can and keep trying to make things work.

We can only make strategies and plans where we can expect that certain things will go our way but cannot expect everything to fall as per what's planned. And with all of this, time is the most important component of the idea of generating wealth and value.

For all those who have tried their hands at timing the stock or financial markets, they have only burnt their hands with it…and you don't really want that to happen to your life, would you?

The cyclical nature of a bullish economy, which includes painful segments of a downward spiral, is similar to a bullish stock that doesn't always move up on all days but moves up in total. Stock trades and life are similar in this manner as well; there are some down days even when we are making progress in total, and it's completely okay and part of the larger game.

More of right and less of wrong, more of positives and less of negatives, more of profits and less of losses with money and life could just be the right balance we are looking for. For no one can be right all the time.

Money provides enough motivation to a host of people, and for some, nothing else remotely interests them. Also, people sometimes get all their motivation from making money while not even spending it at all. They like to sleep over their riches, feel good about it, and keep their quest for more of it despite not knowing what they will spend it on.

That's only fair if that's what they like and plan to do moving forward. If they are happy doing it and, their happiness isn't bound by the ambition of having a certain amount of money in their bank account before they think they can rest and be ecstatic about it forever.

Some people derive happiness from money only by storing the excess of it, and some by buying a variety of things and experiences with it. Yes, money may not be able to buy prolonged emotional stability, but it very well has the power to buy spurts of ecstatic moments involving a lot of things that interest you.

Some who say that money doesn't affect your happiness quotient are likely the ones who haven't experienced an acute shortage of it in their lives. Even if their views are true as per their personal experiences, on the contrary, it does manage to buy you a lot of good moments, and even if you are not happy, that's a better and comfortable state of discontent to stay in.

The current generation is an impatient lot and doesn't believe in saving much, wanting to get-rich-quick to fulfil the whims and fantasies that the consumerist society brings to the table. But what we need to know is that the generation of wealth and its multiplication takes time, and falling for get-rich-quick schemes may leave you at a point of no return.

Although understanding the mindset of the next generation is challenging, educating them about money and its importance early in school can be highly beneficial. It's very surprising that even though making and managing money remains to be the most important aspect of life and survival, hardly anything is taught about it. Even if it's not a comprehensive curriculum, instilling an understanding of the value of money and recognizing the emotions and impulses attached to it can prove to be helpful in the long run.

It's also easy to have those impulses that make you want to spend all that money at your disposal right now. For the life theories that say the present is everything, don't mention that tomorrow also has to be taken care of. And to control those impulses, it's always better to have an accountability system in place that forces us not to be reckless about it. A long-term goal that forces us to be responsible enough or a short-term commitment for a certain amount of what you make going towards different saving and spending budgets. If that's the case, we can spend and indulge in what we want to guilt-free, knowing that all else has been taken care of.

Every phase in life brings some new lessons about the importance of money, be it with our own experiences or with those around us. Most financial defaults are a result of uninsured hefty expenses, overtly and unreasonably ambitious actions during good times taking into account the current and future cash flow, assuming that it will continue, and some due to just plain bad luck or the randomness of the world.

But only when the tide turns, and good times change due to some internal or external factors the finances are exposed and leave the ruins behind.

It's okay to be a bit reckless and aggressive with your approach when you are young since it's only you who is involved and will have to face the result of it. But when you have dependents and responsibilities, it becomes much more important to take calculated risks only.

It's advisable to insure yourself and your assets against possible unfortunate events and also learn from the painful experiences of reckless financial behaviours of others and not allow them to happen to you, as financial failure and not being able to provide for your family is one of the most painful events in this world, especially for those who have only seen the good times till now in their lives.

Also, what you must know is that the most important thing that money can buy for you is time and freedom. Time for you to pursue your passions and interests and have the freedom to spend on things and pursuits related to them.

Sometimes it makes people happy to make more and more money and be able to retain and invest it, but there is a catch.

In spite of having a lot more than that's enough for you and continuing to make more of it, there is a cost associated with it. And that cost is not always monetary; it's the time that you are losing since we all have only finite amount of it and once it's gone you cannot buy that time back under any circumstances.

How much money is enough for you to want to value your time and freedom, more than indulging in making more of it at the cost of what you really want to do and spending time on things that matter to you??

That's for you to decide.

5

Society

How do we decide what is right from wrong?
The good from the bad?
And does a universal right or wrong even exist?

They say it's our conscience, but isn't our present conscience made of belief systems, experiences, and interactions we have had till now? And the beliefs keep changing as per the situations and experiences we find ourselves in and also the extent of our involvement in those scenarios. How is this any different from some of us having a different perspective and for that matter deciding our right and wrong based on our experiences.

Living together in communities, people are expected to follow certain rules and behaviours, but almost every reaction of human behaviour is learned through our experiences which may or may not involve people from only one community. It's when different societies collaborate, different viewpoints are discussed and sometimes followed, it often leads to the dissatisfaction of the current school of thought.

Consider a chessboard as a society where everyone is supposed to play by the rules of the board. The pawn, the king, queen, and everything else must move as per the rules decided for their movement and behaviour, helping in maintaining peace and winning by adhering to what they are supposed to do.

But what if every piece wants to move on their own, and what if some external force wants to allot different movements to some members including the pawns who are dissatisfied with their powers on the board and believe they deserve more and want the power of the Queen?

Since there are more pawns on the board and thus being in the majority, they start to think that one of them deserves to rule the board. The only thing is there are eight of them on one side, and every pawn would then want that topmost place for itself.

And some of them would even want to move away from the board because they believe there is much to explore beyond the board and within other societies where the members have more individuality and opportunities for movements and growth.

Since wherever there is a tight-knit community and groups, there will always be a bias in favour of those who are a part of it and against those aren't. If the constituent pieces or members decide to act independently, the society will descend into chaos or disorder of the highest degree.

"What if a pawn, having defeated the opposite side's queen, then turns against its own queen and claims the throne? Sounds familiar in today's world, doesn't it?"

If it were humans, the black and white pieces on the board would have conspired together by now, based on their colour, movement, power, and positions to suit their personal interests and future prospects, attempting to take over the power dynamics.

It isn't always about the board; it is about the people onboard (pun intended), their ambitions, experiences, and individual thought processes.

But can there be a society where everyone is satisfied and wants to continue the current way forever? Is a board that is free of all biases, always fair towards its members, merely a utopian concept?

In a society, every single piece wishes to have the freedom of movement of its own, or at least some part of it and not be completely bound by the rules.

And for the very reason, should the chessboard or the hands moving the pieces be humbler and more acceptable towards the pieces wanting the way of their own or punish them for wanting to have a mindset different than the majority that will affect the threads of society. Because without these rules, the game of chess wouldn't remain that very game.

Most customs are a way to regulate our behaviour in public and supposedly to guide society on a certain historical, sane path where people follow all the cultures and traditions, for the major decisions in life that are subject to societal scrutiny and acceptance. The ones that can be kept away from the judgement of society are decided based on individual preferences anyway.

Is it really wise to strive for a level playing field for all, or is it more important to keep everyone in line? Or can there be an extent to which deviation from the rules can be allowed?

There are people who don't follow all the principles and teachings of the community and are happy living their lives with a sense of not being bound by anything they cannot relate to.

But the foundation of the community is validated by the interactions between its people.

Without society and community, there would be no common rules to follow, and we may just be running around like headless chickens, not knowing what to do even when having access to the absolute freedom we have always wanted.

And while sometimes we rue that society should allow more freedom of choice, it's also a fact that we cannot live in a world without regulations and people adhering to certain rules and laws of the land and the community leaving everything to individual behaviour and wishes.

It's a paradox where we think we can completely escape society, as some rules are the building blocks of a peaceful community. While it might seem that allowing each individual to act according to their own wishes could lead to prosperity, the problem with anarchy is that it's inherently dangerous.

But the difference lies in the fact that humans always have or develop a sense of belonging, if not at a younger age, then definitely at the later stages of life where they seek the stability of the rules of the board more than the impulses.

All the customs and the regulations may not be a problem for everyone, the unjust ones are. But how do you establish the difference between the just and unjust ones. It may just be the point of view of a smaller group in terms of their personal preferences. Also, some laws are just moral ones, and everyone's morality differs with others and also with their own views at different stages of their feelings, ages, and lives.

If a promise of secrecy accompanies individual decisions, many choices and actions might turn out differently than they would if everyone in the community could observe, judge, and provide feedback.

In democratic times, individuals want societies to be driven by the freedom of choice, even if it's not primarily for the freedom of expression. This includes the ability for individuals to make choices regarding their careers, relationships, and all other aspects of their lives

Every society has some positives and negatives, some truths, and some pretences. Some social beliefs bind people together, while some alienate them.

Though it's always easier to follow certain beliefs when within the system of a particular community, when you are in a group that comprises people of various belief systems, you often act according to interests that may benefit you more than sounding like an ardent follower of your individual belief system which may not go down well with the majority.

You can still be thinking something else underneath, but behavioural plausibility, where there is a mix of belief systems, has become synonymous with being politically correct.

No society has ever been fully just, and it likely will never be because the rules have been made by a group of people at a certain time in history where the circumstances were different, and inclusion was not warranted. And when people are raised that way and have already lived most of their lives believing something, it's unlikely to change that belief overnight.

The narratives we come across in all the descriptions aren't always all-inclusive but more divisive, in which every society wants to project itself as a superior model of operations.

There will always be divisions on the basis of money, status, gender, caste, colour, religion, language, and many more aspects. Some within the society and some intersociety as well. The behaviour, treatment, and privileges of the entities change with respect to these differences.

That's a truth that may take a long, long time to change, or perhaps, in all probability, may never change.

Religion

There isn't a clear and apparent connection between religion and all people being tightly-knit and content., but religious people, by self-admission, consider themselves happier and satisfied with life as they develop a purpose and accountability towards the almighty, while also following the rules of society with it.

This may stem from the fact that devout followers of a belief are more disciplined and feel they have a supreme power which always has their back and whom they can rely upon in times of distress.

And following the routines and beliefs brings comfort and trust that is indirectly responsible for a calmer mind and life. Also, with the religious events and gatherings, people tend to make better friends of similar wavelength and seem to have found a purpose of life in serving the community from one common platform.

And when you feel that there are a lot of people who share your concerns and thoughts and the short and long-term goals, you get the confidence and mental strength to face the process while also following the broader mandate that's prescribed by society.

We had heard about Ikigai or the purpose of life. It can be of the individual or of a society or a community at large. It is when both of these align, i.e., the purpose of the majority individuals aligns with the historical purpose of society, the confluence creates a better situation overall for societal stability.

It also isn't necessary to have a similar connection to society all your life; there can be little or a complete disconnect from the herd when we are young, and it can also convert to complete dependence for the sense of direction and belonging when at the later stages of life.

Reasoning isn't always important. Some traditions are being followed only for the reason that they have been since ages, and it's considered bad omen to break those traditions, and since the elders have always asked us to follow these.

Everything cannot be correlated with science and tech, and the belief systems matter a lot more sometimes than the reality or the truth. Societies may have a few such which may not have any reason and may seem irrational or redundant yet following them without reason may just be the thread that binds people together.

Many religions believe in the law of karma and reincarnation, and many don't. But what is it that's true? Since we are all the same, there can only be one theory that holds water.

Again, half the world population doesn't believe in reincarnation as per their religious beliefs, and some do believe that we reap what we sow in this life only, and it does not carry forward to the next.

Is there really an afterlife or reincarnation for that matter? As per what they say, it's your karma that will decide where you will end up based on all the good and bad that has been done by us in the current and the previous lives. The people who have done more right than wrong may end up in a better situation than those who've done otherwise.

Which half of the world is right and the wrong? And if there isn't reincarnation or afterlife, the fear of the judgement day or being born again in an abject situation, why is it taught to some and not to others.

If the destiny and the life process are already written, how does the karma aspect work? And if your karma is affected by a multitude of factors and other individuals, how are we only responsible for the effects of it?

Sometimes we consider the existence of a chart that details specific planetary alignments at the time of your birth, indicating potential aspects and possibilities throughout your entire lifetime with a certain probability. In the Indian marriage system, horoscopes of two people are matched to assess the compatibility of the involved and predict if the marriage will be successful.

There are reasons why it's considered important, one is to follow the traditions since it's been the process for generations, and to ensure that a probable aspect of creating a balanced marriage isn't left out only for it to be noticed later.

The readings believe that the place and time of birth, the positions of planets hold strong influence over what happens in our lives, and any potential problems in the future can be avoided if the process is followed and some aspects are taken care of.

But what if there are two individuals who want to spend their lives together, but their birth charts don't match?

In one culture, it's considered sacred, while others refuse to believe in the authenticity of the predictions, citing their different experiences and also probably owing to the belief that God is in control of everything and whatever is to happen has already been decided. They believe that whatever happens in our lives is meant to happen irrespective of whatever we do, believe, and also regardless of the positions of planets and the places and time of birth.

Some people believe in God, and some do not. But since the beginning of humanity, people have believed in a higher power. The wonders of life, mysteries of the universe, and creation of living beings with so much thought and practicality cannot just be the result of adaptation and evolution alone. All this stuff seems completely inexplicable and also beyond human control, thus obviously enticing the people to believe in the existence of a supreme power.

The desire to connect with that unknown power and find the true meaning of one's existence led the human race towards the concept of religion, the study of the planets, and the stars, believing it to be the way to meet the divine power and follow their preachings as a society. Since every other group had a different image of the supreme power and also the ideas which were perceived for the betterment of society as a whole, multiple religions and beliefs evolved with time, and the teachings of which were inculcated in the religious and sacred books based on the understandings of people who wrote them then at that point in time. The different religions have provided the code of ethics to which the ardent followers must adhere to in order for them to achieve their true purpose of life and karma.

Some people follow almost all the religious practices, worship the planets and stars so as to get rid of their sins; some follow them to do good deeds, and some follow it for emotional support and have some divine power to fall back to and rely upon for ultimate support and also to find courage during tough times. Some just have that ingrained in their mind because they believe life has no meaning without the religious practices and following what it preaches.

But the question remains:

Should the scriptures and studies be reinterpreted owing to the evolution of society? But then they being divine should not be, as most would say. But how can we maintain that the way they were interpreted and are perceived right now is correct in the first place?

A lot of effort goes into passing on the teachings and tenets of the religion and our relations with the heavenly bodies to the next generations in its original form so that the belief system of a society stays intact. Religious families raise their children to follow the same traditions and rituals and have the same beliefs and try to teach them that from a very young age. Although any religion most of the time promotes faith over science and logic, still its role in human development as a society is substantial. Shared religious beliefs bring people together and sometimes even motivate them to work towards a common cause beneficial to their society and community as a whole.

But where does that leave those who believe in the religion and its teachings but want to not apply some of the beliefs which are not acceptable to them? Since as per them, it was way back in times that these scriptures were written, and certain rituals and beliefs are not in line with the current times.

Or someone who is not even sure about the existence of the supreme power and wants to know more before perceiving something written in the scriptures as absolute truth.

People follow or belong to a particular religion due to their lineage of being born in a family following a certain religion. Most continue to follow the same while some become agnostic, and some choose to be atheists at later stages of their life owing to their reasons and experiences in life.

It's really not about verifying the presence of that supreme power but about accepting the coexistence of different belief systems together. Not about which is better and more powerful but about how different societies can add value to each other. Not about calculating the effects of the positions of the planets and the stars but about accepting the uncertainty that comes with it.

If there is or could be a common teaching across all religions, it's not of all peace, but it probably should be the one that teaches them to treat people of all religions as you want to be treated yourself. There will be conflicts as there has always been, but the priority has to always be a peaceful resolution of the differences.

A community cannot always remain peaceful while the other does not; it's a chessboard, after all. Not even the Gods, if we believe what's written in the scriptures, have suggested being completely peaceful, and it's important to be ready to take a different route if the need arises.

Though no one has seen the Almighty since they say it's only after life the soul gets to meet it, sometimes we do feel the intangible presence of God when we believe that there is someone having our back in difficult times, someone to fall back on and be our support system when it's all dark.

The supreme power cannot change from one generation to another, for it remains to be the ultimate truth. Even if it is not, still the very belief keeps us grounded in an ever-changing scenario.

Gone is the time when we only belonged to one society or culture. Today, we are exposed to multiple groups and communities depending on our place of birth, work, inclinations, or interests. Intersocietal influences are common, where people adjust their behaviour and views in accordance with the group they are representing at different times and situations and also while sometimes impulsively switching the herd they belong to be in accordance or to suit their current disposition and interests.

A lot of traditions that used to be followed are being challenged by the current fast-paced generations, some for rational reasons and some for the mere fact that it no longer interests them or doesn't fall into their scheme of things.

And since it's true that many rules and guidelines no longer remain valid pertaining to changing times, the fabric of the society must adapt in order to keep it relevant or else risk going obsolete. The only way that remains is to let go of the bias towards old traditions that may no longer add value and reinvent or allow the change that would eventually have to be made way for.

Changes can't be instantaneous and may take a long time to implement and be accepted. Most often, there will be resistance to change, for it's difficult for the people who have followed certain beliefs all their lives to let go.

The reforms don't always require a revolution, and sometimes acceptance also remains to be a plausible route to it. Agreement with the fact that the world has and will always continue to change, and the beliefs that are being followed since ages may no longer hold the same value to the coming generations is the only way for the bearers of the societal norms to be at peace with the times and themselves.

And if we can inculcate it into our conventional education system and teach the generations the acceptance towards change and that it's inevitable in any form of life and society, that feeling and mindset alone could be enough to allow a better life to take its course, and the sync between the generations. That the beliefs can be changed for the better, sometimes keeping the basic tenets the same, by allowing inclusivity and freedom.

For a community should always hold a sense of acceptance for every member and that's only possible by allowing the individuals the space to act as per their learned belief systems. The sense of belonging only brings us closer, and it's the symbiosis of the old and the new that can only take us forward for the better.

This is the best we can do since both stability and change remain to be important aspects. The symphony of the old and the new making way for gradual change so as not to affect the threads of society.

We remain to be a part of the herd, and as individuals, we need a sense of belonging to survive which in many situations is more useful to us than pursuing the actual truth of the matter.

As goes the famous saying, "For the strength of the pack is the wolf, and the strength of the wolf is the pack."

✳ ✳ ✳

6

Mindset

"Sometimes it's easier to keep going. What's difficult,
though, is to start.
While most of the time, it's the other way around.
And almost always it's all in the mind.

At one moment, the mind can be thinking of one thing and something completely different at the next. It keeps jumping from one to another towards the possibilities and the doubts, sometimes remotely related to the situations we are in at that very moment.

And while a clear mind can be your greatest asset and help you focus on priorities at hand, an anxious or cluttered thought process can make it extremely difficult for you to decide and execute anything at all.

The human mind is a complex maze of thoughts, and navigating through it effectively is impossible unless it is trained to align all the information it has about a certain prospect in order to make decisions. Also, if there is too much information, it becomes harder to arrive at a consensus with all that we know.

What the mind believes is possible or not is, again, a net sum of what has been learned through years of our existence, and it's up to us to channel it towards the results we want.

What if we choose to steer clear of negative thoughts and only concentrate on the positives, considering that everything has those two sides anyway? Or is it even possible to do that? Would life be better if we consistently viewed the glass as half full and disregarded the other half?

Probably yes, but it's sometimes important to know how to respond to the things sent to destroy your peace and mindset intentionally. How to take the negatives aspects of things and be okay with ignoring them and sticking to the positives. It's like mostly residing in a zone defined by a positive state of mind, where you choose to consider the negatives solely as feedback for improvement and move ahead with the positives of everything.

For if your mind is free to take its own course and not made to think otherwise, the negative emotions and thoughts can last for a lifetime, and with that the ability to do a lot of things you have the potential for, would also take a hit.

While it can be challenging to maintain a positive outlook in a negative environment, one strategy is to intentionally choose your surroundings. Additionally, by minimizing exposure to negativity and being open to embracing even the smallest positives, we can cultivate a more optimistic mindset.

The positive frame of mind is a way of life in which we choose our company, our surroundings, and everything else that fits the vibe we want to propagate and receive. And if we learn to do that continuously, you'll be surprised to see how many pieces of the life puzzle start to fit in, which earlier would've seemed impossible.

As they say, 'people around you are either your circle or your cage.'

Maintaining the clarity of mind to think clearly in any situation and selectively accepting only what aligns with our intentions is the first step towards cultivating a healthier mindset. This, in turn, enables us to perceive things at face value and make better decisions.

As Master Oogway says in the movie "Kung Fu Panda", "Your mind is like water, my friend, when it is agitated, it becomes difficult to see, but if you allow it to settle, the answers become clear."

And it's when that's clear: what we think, how we make sense of the world around us, and how we behave and respond to situations determines where and with what we end up in life.

Ideas vs Execution

Good thoughts and ideas are ubiquitous, but it is the execution of an idea, the act of turning it from an intangible thing to reality, is much harder than the thought itself. The idea may have the potential, but it's the execution of that potential that makes all the difference.

When the Android Play Store and the iOS App Store were launched, everyone had great app ideas. However, whenever they tried to pursue them, they often found that someone else had already implemented similar concepts. No matter how many random ideas we can come up with, with the current abundance of information, it would already be taken.

People call it a chicken and egg discussion, but in the true sense, the idea itself isn't worth much;

execution is everything. Everyone can have a brilliant idea, but not everyone possesses the traits for proper execution. If you have a good idea, in all probability, a lot of other people have already thought of the same idea while you are obsessing over that next big groundbreaking idea and the riches that will follow the execution.

Also, ideas are not fully formed initially; they evolve and take shape through execution, often incorporating significant changes based on feedback and responses along the way

A great idea executed badly probably has no chance. Although a weak idea can be compensated to a certain extent by brilliant execution. It's the execution that decides the actual worth of an idea and not the other way round.

No, it doesn't mean the idea isn't important at all. Having a firm belief in what you are executing is crucial because it guides your actions and decisions, influencing the outcome of how well the idea is executed, and also in order to persevere with it even in hard times and even when everything seems to be going haywire..

While it's easy for entrepreneurs to always be looking for that once-in-a-lifetime idea or the latest internet innovation, it's a reality that most people start by replicating existing ideas, and businesses either by making improvements, sometimes competing with existing entities in the same demographics and sometimes somewhere they don't have to deal with the Unicorns.

You can find a lot of examples where a "legendary" company was neither the first one to coin an idea nor the first one to try and execute it. They just executed the already existing idea better either by keeping it the same or by making small changes to it.

Before Facebook, there were Myspace and Orkut, Yahoo was dominant before Google, and Internet Explorer preceded Chrome; Apple didn't invent the smartphone, but they executed it better than anyone else.

Flipkart and Baazee.com (later acquired by eBay) were founded in India in 2000, operating along similar lines as Amazon.com in the US. It's worth noting that Amazon launched in India only in 2016.

Also, the failure of an idea doesn't always invalidate it. Advantage of having a benchmark model to work on is that you can apply some of its failures and learnings and better your product as per the current times before you launch to compete.

Or you can also go ahead with a similar model and launch in a different demographic, fine-tuned to the local conditions and customer expectations and preferences.

If you wish to start from scratch and develop your own unique product, then the execution of the idea must accompany the details of what your target audience is and how and where you plan to sell it.

But if the idea, when executed, starts to generate the response you intend, many other companies will dive in with much more resources and a stronger workforce and take the icing on the cake in most cases. In current times, it's becoming tougher to execute good original ideas without being confronted by a massively funded opposition. Also, the first mover has to put extra effort into creating the demand for the product, while the ones launched after that may already have estimated the market's demand and took a plunge based on the consumer response to the innovator's venture.

Sometimes, individuals will have the same ideas but then move on to execute them in a completely different way, resulting in a completely different end product.

The reason for different outcomes would be the different sets of thoughts, experiences, strategies, and hurdles they would've faced while executing the idea. Also, one rendition may yield good results, and the other may not, though the seed idea remains the same. Some will fail, and some will do good, and only a few will go on to do exceptional things. Still, for those who are willing to learn from their mistakes and want to keep trying, even when the original plan doesn't work, the experiences of the journey can lead them to better ideas or execution methods.

Also, it's pretty clear that most people do not have the traits to execute their ideas and some of them settle to make a career out of critical evaluation of those who do. After all, it's very easy to find faults while sitting in a rocking chair, in a nice office, having to execute nothing but find faults in everything and write about what should have been done in hindsight.

Movie critics seem to know all the details and nuances regarding the film-making process, but have you ever thought that if they know so much about it, why don't they make one? Since, by what they depict in their articles and critical reviews of a movie, they seem to know what should've been done and where the movie has gone wrong. In a sense, if they venture into movie making, then chances are that they will deliver a string of blockbusters since nothing could go wrong with it.

But obviously, the execution is a different project altogether, and it's a complex and an arduous task. Some critics who have tried filmmaking have only burnt their hands at it and gone back to what they do best, advising and pointing out faults. The easiest thing to do in the world, isn't it?

There have been movies or artworks bashed by the experts which ended up making a lot of money because it was received well by the end consumer or the audience.,

As it is, there is no good or bad movie per one single person; it's the audience that decides what they want to watch. In similar terms, the buyers of the idea decide whether the execution of it is useful to them or not for them to spend their hard-earned money on it. There just has to be enough of them for you to make good money out of your idea.

* * *

Ideas can be big or small, varying in terms of location and size, and tailored to specific segments and strategies. They don't have to be patented, never-before-heard, once-in-a-lifetime concepts.

Opening a Preschool in a new society can be a good idea, Manufacturing the goods locally when they are being imported can be a good idea, and also the change in marketing and sales strategy and positioning your current product range or expanding the availability to new areas can be a good idea if the execution is viable and properly done.

There is another aspect to the impending execution of your ideas, i.e., if you have strategic expertise over your competition in the domain. Or are you aware of the risks and chaos that are going to accompany the execution process? The idea could have a huge potential, but small executions and accomplishments of constituent modules also play a very important part in the continuous motivation towards achieving the final frontier.

There is also a third dimension to the discussion towards which you have no control, the 'luck' factor or good or bad fortune, which some individuals seem to have an explicable abundance of when compared to others as already discussed, the outcome of an event can be random, working either in your favour or against you. While many people believe in luck, whether good or bad, there are also many who do not, or at least have not had experiences that have led them to believe in it.

Looking at examples all around the world and how the luck factor has changed the lives of many by delivering the outcomes over which they had no control at all, there is a consensus among the majority that it does have a role to play in whatever we do and have, and only the ratio of it in the contribution towards the happening of the outcome changes.

Some say the harder and smarter you work, the luckier you get; not everyone will agree with it, though.

Perfectionism

Many great ideas never see the light of day.

The reason for this lies more in our mindset than in our actual capability to execute them.

A lot of people spend a lot of time trying to perfect something before they actually do it.

You must've heard of the term, and while most of us would believe that it's good to have that trait of perfectionism, many would argue that this is, in fact, a hindrance in pursuing the execution of the ideas swiftly.

It's defined as a desire to behave and execute everything in its perfect form, in which a person sets very high-performance standards and expects flawlessness; it also subjects itself to continuous critical self-evaluations. It evolves from a feeling of telling yourself that you will be judged for every little mistake you make, and you won't get another opportunity if you make errors.

Yes, we all want to be well-prepared and well-versed in all the details of what we are about to execute, but we cannot just keep waiting for that perfect time and preparation levels. The trait is also accompanied by the fear of failure and being at your perfect self before taking the plunge.

A perfectionist's goals are not always even reasonable, and since they get disappointed easily by nothing less than perfection, it's a fast and enduring track to dissatisfaction and unfulfilled goals.

It is driven by the desire to avoid failures or being judged by others in a negative manner, and that's why it drives you to be very cautious regarding the execution of your ideas. Even a small mistake made makes you critical of yourself for a very long time as you vow to not repeat it the next time.

It's like telling yourself that you are not good enough yet and need to prepare more in order to do better or be acceptable, and it often drives you to mundane tasks where you can put off the work related to your primary goal and stick to manual distractions so that you can buy more time to prepare more for being that perfect version of yourself.

Also, you end up devoting so much time to fine-tuning the small irrelevant details which would not even matter to most of the people who are to view your work, which also leaves you with a mental block that requires you to devote a substantially greater amount of time to a task than required.

How often do we see a video, a dance move, or a speech delivered in front of an audience and believe that we could've done it better? But when the time comes, we develop cold feet and wish we had more time to prepare and start blaming the circumstances.

You also start to have high expectations from others, and this causes frustration as you have trouble trusting anyone to get things done right and feel that something will surely go wrong in case of your absence. All of this ends up with you trying to do most things yourself.

The only catch is that the time takes too long to come, and it leads to procrastination, a dreaded word that implies delaying a certain task until it becomes very urgent or not doing it at all while focusing on less important things.

There is an old adage, namely Parkinson's Law, which says that work will expand to fill the time allotted for its completion.

It's not easy to avoid the pattern unless you figure out a way to do it for yourself, probably by setting shorter deadlines and accountability methods.

But what if there is no time allotted or there is no deadline? And we can do it whenever we want to, taking whatever amount of time we can.

Or assume that it's okay even if it's not done at all. Well, we could do that if something is not a compulsion. However, there is a catch.

"Not having that deadline and procrastinating indefinitely, that's where most of life's regrets start to originate from."

When we want to do and be a lot of things in life, for which we believe we have the potential and temperament, but we find ourselves in a zone where there are no deadlines or accountability. We can do it whenever we want since there seems to be plenty of time, but in reality, there isn't.

The time available is the same for everyone, the same 60 minutes an hour and 24 hours a day. And it keeps ticking as we keep thinking about that perfect moment to start, to learn a bit more to be better at it.

Soon, before you even realise it, you are stuck in situations or at an age where it's not possible for you to do it anymore. And it very well starts to turn into a regret of the lifetime.

We always have a chance at becoming what we believe we can, only if we can persevere enough and if the mind allows us to, owing to the complex ways it works. Sometimes, it doesn't even seem like it's in our control due to the complex emotions and thoughts it keeps generating."

We need to stop devoting time to executions that are not useful to our ultimate goals. It's always good to hire professional help for what you believe you are not good at or something that will take a lot of time to learn while redundant to your long-term goals and devote more time to the core of what you want to do.

We all make mistakes, and that's okay. It's our imperfections that make life interesting. If you keep dreaming about that perfect day and that perfect moment and level of preparation when you will start what you have always wanted to, it is now. Take the plunge and improve on the way to your destination because life isn't going to wait for you; it keeps slipping away.

Start executing your ideas, accept failure, learn from mistakes, and start again. That's life for you. All of this obviously leaves some room for improvement, for ideas have a very limited shelf life, and waiting indefinitely for the situation and preparations to be perfect isn't advisable as you may lose a lot of opportunities due to the unwarranted evaluations.

The truth is still the same as we started with that 'it's all in the mind'. Starting to execute anything may not be that difficult once you have made up your mind, but what's hard is to decide and stick to it.

Decoding the state of Shunya, or zero, represents a mindset that can enhance how you navigate life. It involves being present in the moment, thinking clearly, free from bias and emotions. This state can also help you become immune to the emotions and impulses that push for perfection before beginning anything, and it can also alleviate the fear of failure and judgment

It is akin to maintaining a positive attitude towards everything by rejecting all negatives and enabling the mind to erase redundant thoughts, returning to its original state that in turn also helps avoid the feeling of inertial perfectionism.

If we decide to achieve a state of mind where it's all calm and there is no chaos, it becomes very important to promote order in our daily life at first in general because that's where all of it begins.

"It's essential to declutter the basics in life, starting with the most fundamental aspects. This could include your work desk or your bookshelf, among others. Small changes and habits can truly make a difference, especially since you don't want to begin your day surrounded by clutter, which is precisely what you're trying to eliminate. Additionally, once clutter triggers your thought process, it can take time to return to normal."

Chaos anywhere can cause us to lose focus, even if It's in and around the mind, and only the organized and the calm state of mind knows what it wants and also what it should and should not respond to, what to believe and what not to, avoiding the chaos and the negative feedback of the world around.

If you could believe that you can, it's probable that you will have a good shot at it.

Most things happen in this world if you believe; it's also the start of so many great things once we get into that frame of mind. And since our thoughts have the potential to make or destroy us, it's important to avoid the mind letting us tell anything other than believing in the possibilities. That's what makes your mind and how it thinks the most important asset and aspect of how you want to shape your life. Everything that we do originates from that single thought that we choose to continue thinking upon and not forget as a whim.

'You just need to believe. You must believe,' a famous movie quote said.

7

Success

Can we define success in absolute terms?
Probably not.
Is every success accompanied by happiness?
Certainly not.

Absolute or Relative, success seems like an abstract concept, difficult to define. And it's different for everyone else and moreover takes different forms at different stages of life.

Everyone wants to be successful in life, but exactly what kind of successful do you want to be in life? Your success or society's success, what you believe would make you happy or what you want to achieve as a reply to the naysayers. For society, money is the primary measure of success at the outset, and fame may qualify as a close second. All else other than these may not even matter to the uninformed.

In prevalent success models, the chances and odds in favour are less, and competition is much higher. The availability of a level playing field or equal opportunities is even rarer. Furthermore, the due to the presence of even more variables, role of luck is as random as it has ever been.

Since an early age, we are taught to be ambitious and work towards a successful life. Our parents expect us to be more successful and also achieve a lot more than they did in their lives. But does the perceived success, relative or absolute, make us as happy as we want to be, or does it take much more than that?

Also, sometimes, the perceived success brings a lot of suffering, and we wish that we could go back and not continue to be in that place or position.

The only catch here is that the definition of success varies from person to person and also depending on their present circumstances. Someone might appear successful to an outsider, while they might be at their unhappiest self at all times.

What do you consider to be the ingredients of success? Money, fame, position, or authority? But remember, when you already have or achieve these, your definition of success would've already changed to an extent, and then you would want to have more than what you have right now.

Yes, you can continue to rest on your laurels, but it won't keep providing you the satisfaction it once did forever. It's a never-ending journey where one success doesn't cut it for long, and we must move on to the next to keep being successful in our minds and stay relevant, as per the classic definition of it.

The thing with these parameters of a perceived success story is that you never have enough. The lure of the lucre and power is that the more you have, the more you want. More money, more power, and more authority, and the quest continues forever.

Being financially independent and having access to all the basics of life is an absolute necessity, but beyond a certain point, you cannot directly link having more of these to being happier than those having less of it.

A person who lives in a small house and wants to buy a big one considers it a big success when it happens. If a person who doesn't have a television in the house buys one, he considers himself successful. On the other hand, a millionaire who wants to buy a private jet may consider himself unworthy unless he is able to buy one. There is always a mirage waiting on the other side that, in spite of having everything, coerces you towards having more.

You would remember that in childhood when you were allowed to write with a pencil only, you wanted that mighty pen to write with, also, when you wanted to grow up quickly, citing a lot of things you would be allowed to do when it happens.

But when all this happened, did that mean a thing, or it just left you feeling the same or worse? It probably would've appeared to be a step backwards from being your happy self, as in the process of achieving anything that we want, a lot of unwanted scenarios and chaos interfere with the peace of mind that we wanted success to accompany in the first place. You tend to want a certain thing or event to happen, but how long does that keep you feeling successful or keep you happy, for that matter… not eternally, for sure.

You have been looking to buy a dream sedan car for years, reading about it, learning its specifications, reading reviews, choosing your favourite colour, and the possible routes that you will travel to when you buy one. But how long does it actually keep you happy or interested when you have one, a week or a month at most, maybe a bit longer. But the world is like that, and every success is just a phase, temporary or prolonged but never permanent.

Also, citing a few examples of ultra-rich achievers and wealthy individuals whom we perceive as always happy and successful due to their achievements and the money they have at their disposal, when you monitor closely, only then you are able to see the shortcomings in their life; they have their set of problems too and sometimes a lot more than the average person. And while they may not have to worry about where their next meal will come from, they certainly have a lot of other aspects to deal with.

Also, while you may consider them successful because they can buy and have everything in the world, they might not be considered to be such amongst their peers who will be equally powerful and rich when compared to each other.

As you move up that path and as you gain fame, fortune, and seniority, people will treat you better, they will hold doors open for you, and while this is not true for your individual self but more for the position you are at and for the assets you possess, this will still continue as long as you stay relevant to the involved people.

As you move on the success ladder, your social circle changes, and it keeps changing with every positive and negative movement in the achievement graph. Your current position decides who you share the dinner table with and who you have those business and knowledge sessions with. And while you were very successful compared to your previous peers, you suddenly find yourself as part of the crowd after this new uptick.

And again, you are faced with renewed expectations, insecurities of falling back to the previous level, anxiousness about proving yourself amongst the peers, and sometimes with all of this, you even start to think you were better off earlier.

Success in some form of achievement, money, or power also brings in a barrage of friends who want to benefit from you in the long-term. The social circle keeps on increasing when you are on a successful spree and keeps on diminishing when it reverses.

The social strata in today's world are defined by money and position, and no one wants to be socially connected with a non-achiever or who, in some or another, cannot be of benefit to one.

Also, more importantly, it is imperative to stay relevant for your loved ones throughout your life if you want to be loved. Yes, strange as it may sound today, the world has already come to this. Staying relevant to your kids, your spouse, staying relevant to your social circle is important because if you do not, then even the closest people to you will forget you on a whim.

Being of no use to anyone is especially painful when you look back at your life and see a whole lot of good things you have done for people, and when at this time you cannot contribute as you once did, you would find that you have suddenly lost a majority of your circle.

That doesn't always mean that you should stop being ambitious or stop working; climbing the social ladder is an utmost important part of one's life, and it makes you go through great experiences workwise and in relationships, personal and professional as well.

It's also important to savour your small wins on the way to that big win you are looking for, be in love with the process, and find happiness in those moments alongside that hustle. If you could just celebrate the small moments along the way, the potential for creating lifelong memories is immense.

You shouldn't wait for that promotion to celebrate with your kids since they will be grown-ups soon;

you cannot wait for that car to celebrate with your parents since they may not be around anymore when that happens.

There isn't a perfect time for everything in life, and it's better to live it as it comes because if you keep waiting for it to reach a certain perfect point to execute those ecstatic moments you have planned, you may realise that the reason for it or the people you wanted to celebrate it aren't with you anymore.

There is no ultimate destination where you will be eternally happy. Even people with a lot of money and power tend to get bored and anxious with the stability and stagnation of life and want something new to look forward to in order to be happy. It's about not being inertial and continuing to move forward, as change is the only constant that can keep you interested in life.

A famous person in a TED talk said, "If you expect little from life, you will get a little from life. If you do what the majority does, you will have what the majority have, which usually isn't much. And if you want to be successful in life and are willing to travel that path, you may just end up getting what you want. But for that, you have to keep moving and embracing the change.

"At times, people who discover happiness feel happy after giving up the pursuits they have dedicated their life to. For when they reach their destination, they could see that it means very little."

If your success is not associated with happiness, then you may be wasting your time by just wearing it as a badge of honour for the society, since like everyone else, your time is limited here.

It's easier to get lost in the thoughts of what we haven't done till now and of a lot more that we need to get done and it's that mindset that makes us feel disappointed with our efforts in spite of knowing that we can never do all of what we want to and also what others expect us to.

There is a difference between being successful and feeling successful, and while the first depends upon the conventional definition of it or more of what others perceive it to be, the latter is what is most important as per what we make out of it.

Failure

If we have discussed success, it becomes very important to discuss failure as well because, without the failures, there wouldn't be much success to celebrate and talk about.

The courage to do something unconventional is seen as stupidity at first, but when it starts to take shape in a good way, it is then that it starts to be seen as wise. And if it doesn't work out, all we could hear is that it was a pretty bad idea to begin with.

The word failure is commonly associated with a negative undertone but is often an undermined yet unavoidable tool that when used to our advantage, has enough lessons and opportunities of growth through learning and possible improvements.

The inability to meet our expectations with something we are emotionally attached to sometimes makes us consider it a failure to such an extent that we cannot get over it. And those moments come with feelings that are difficult to handle. We could try not to have those emotions every time we fail, but it's not really our prerogative.

Expecting something to play out exactly how we had imagined it to happen very rarely and mostly turns into disappointment when the time comes. And when that happens, the mind keeps going back to what we could have done better and what could have been avoided to change what has already happened. That judgement of the process that has already taken its course does a lot of damage.

Because, like everything else, the number of times we have been right doesn't matter, but that one failure in the pursuit of something we have always aspired towards has an effect on our entire lives.

It is important to recognize that the result of an effort isn't always entirely in our hands. In times where competition in every field is immense, the possibility of failure is much higher. For this reason, we need to start normalizing failure so that it doesn't affect us in a destructive way. If not for failures, difficult experiences can be the best thing that can happen to you, as they teach us how to deal with unpleasant situations.

Think of someone that you consider as successful and happy in their life.

You are free to do it as per your definition of success, which may include fame, money, privacy (yes, that is a prized feat these days), material possessions, contacts, or power or someone who gets to earn well while following their passion.

Any scientist, any actor, any businessman, any politician before they have reached that stage of perceived success would have undoubtedly had their fair share of failures, big or small, in pursuit of the position and in the journey to where they are today.

Failure can be small or big, comparative or absolute, redundant or important. 'Whatever the odds are in favour, we fail on a daily basis, sometimes multiple times in a day in doing the numerous tasks at hand.'

When we fail, we get disappointed, ponder over them for some time, maybe take a break and do things that interest us for a while to gain our sanity back and then get back to living again. And living by itself involves failures at large on a daily basis.

The more we fail in our early years, the better it is for a prolonged successful life, as those failures humble us in many ways and make us understand that everything is fallible and not everything we touch will turn to gold.

As kids, we often experience failure while trying to ride a bike for the first time, learning to walk, swim, write, or attempting anything and everything, for that matter."

Then why do we start to hate failing or become so averse to it that we sometimes end up not even trying what we want to do or achieve in life for fear of failure and being judged?

Probably because we start to value the feedback we receive once we attain social status and also become scared of getting negative ones rather than welcoming them for the sake of improvements. When we step out of our comfort zone, we often enter uncharted territory and feel cautious about feedback, fearing potential mistakes.

That fear of feedback for the pretending perfectionists results in a form of procrastination which forces us into an inertia that may even result in destroying the potential we may have had for much bigger things.

For the world, all eyes are on the winners, and those who fail don't get much to celebrate about, except for what they could learn from those experiences and then improve by using those lessons. On the contrary, sometimes those who lose are even belittled and made fun of.

In the context of today where everyone is on social media boasting of their successful moments and high lives, the theory of accepting the failures becomes even more important. To realise that life cannot be perfect, and it is only the failures that make success make us feel the way it does.

Due to the fact that every single one of us faces stiff competition across all walks of life and chances of perceived success are very minuscule, it's important to stay sane even after a streak of unsuccessful trials.

Only if we could normalise the term failure while we teach the kids the importance of it and more important aspects of how to deal with it, while we always emphasise on the successful stories, the details of the efforts and failures can inspire everyone more.

The current and the next are a vulnerable generation, are scared of failures and also of being ridiculed for it, which in turn is causing emotional chaos amongst them.

Only if we could see the failure resumes of famous and successful people and assess their life journey first-hand, we would know that someone could have failed all their life and have a failure list much bigger than that of the successes they had mentioned on their resume and what they are considered successful for.

That there is still hope even after a string of failures and, not everything is lost and possibilities for better always exist doesn't matter what stages of life you are at.

That you can still be enjoying those little joys that come your way while trying for that goal you want to achieve.

It is often said that success is a journey and not a destination, and that remains true for all forms of success as you have to work much harder to maintain the level of success that you've attained in your life since you have to keep delivering consistent results.

If you are familiar with the term relative velocity, you would know that the only difference between speed and velocity is that the latter denotes the speed of an object with respect to the other.

If both objects are moving in the same direction, their relative speed patterns will appear slower than the actual speed or progress.

Whatever we do, we may appear slower or faster to others than our actual speed of progress and growth, depending upon how they view it and in what direction they are moving.

And more of this, if we choose to believe it, will tell us that there is nothing absolute about anyone's success or failure. Some people want fame and publicity as success, and some people pay a lot of money to safeguard their privacy after they are famous and rich. Some earn a lot of money but cannot find their way out of that infinite loop of responsibilities to make use of that money.

All of it, when looked from a distance, looks very enticing and makes us believe that it's all that is required to live a good and happy life.

But as they say, 'The grass isn't always greener on the other side; it's greener where you choose to water it.'

But, since in today's world, most of the success, failure, and growth scenarios are measured relative to someone else's data of the same parameters, it becomes very important to know the difference between absolute and relative failure, both of which entirely depends upon how you choose to see it. The same event can be taken as a success and failure at the same time depending upon how you look at it.

When you come second in a sporting event, you failed to grab that first place, but it still is a success in a lot of ways, and it gives you motivation to work towards that one step you need to move up towards.

There have been successful people (sports personalities, artists, businessmen) who have spent their lives in discontent because, as per them, they had failed to reach a certain level of success they deserved or had potential for. That level they had set their eyes on to decide on their definition of success mostly is marked with respect to someone who already has touched that level of it.

There may be a lot of reasons why you may feel like having failed at a lot of things, but most of them will be derived out of comparison with other people and situations and also from what you believe you should have achieved and could not, and in any way, that cannot be absolute.

Though the extent of it does take a toll on us emotionally, in life, it is very important for us to know what failures feel like and how to cope with them, as only these experiences can pave the path of growth personally and professionally for us.

Just like success isn't final, failure also isn't absolute until you give up the prospects of progress completely.

Failures make us humble and stronger, and they result in a process where we can figure out easier ways of doing difficult things by solving problems on a regular basis while facing small failures on a path to bigger success.

What you are at present is the result of experiences shaped by a series of failures, emotional breakdowns, and constant rejections of things you believed you worked hard for and deserved. Enduring such challenges can transform you into someone capable of achieving your desired level of success and maintaining it over the long term. This journey also builds the mental courage and stamina needed to handle the positives and negatives that come with success.

No event is a failure for a person who believes in their potential and is willing to work for it. While it does bring the risks of its own, once you are comfortable with the idea of failure, it would stop affecting you much, and you will develop coping mechanisms that suit your temperament to come out of the after-effects of any unfavourable event with a better mindset and outlook. When the same situation arises again, you would know how to respond like a battle-ready body and mind if you have learned enough from that past event.

When you grow up and look back at the things that deeply affected you at certain points in your life—whether related to age, career, or relationships—you'll find that they wouldn't matter as much to you if they happened now.

What you will see, though, is that multiple failures led to one big success; what you will see is that all the comparisons that made you feel that you were failing were redundant.

If you are feeling angry, disappointed, and disheartened with the small failures now, you don't need to. You just need to grow an understanding of how all of this works and that such events are inevitable.

If you did your best, that was all you could do, since everything else was beyond your control. Yes, it could've gone your way, but that could just be hope for every time we try, for things to go our way and random instances of luck to favour us to add to all of the efforts that we made.

It's important to treat the failures as the stepping stones of your growth objective and embrace the learnings for future endeavours. For if we don't move forward, we would always remain at the same place. And if we stay stagnant, all that could go wrong will go wrong.

For all those who procrastinate indefinitely, the question remains the same: Do you want to be someone who is afraid of failures for the fear of reactions, being judged, or ridiculed, or someone who loves success and will treat the failures on the way as the apparatus and mediums to achieve what you want to?

We should rather choose the latter and take failure in our stride, for if we don't, life will slowly pass by, and looking back at it and being regretful over what we could've achieved in life would not cut it in any way.

We, and the others always have and would continue to fail. The failures are what make our life interesting as they challenge us to surpass our best versions, push us to make that extra effort, and move out of our comfort zones to achieve that little bit of extra that everyone always seems to want from their lives.

Failure remains to be an obvious part of our existence, and only when we are open to going wrong can we truly open up and start to explore opportunities around. It's important to treat failures as a natural outcome and not get too attached or affected by them and stop trying for the results that you want to achieve.

Whatever happens in the world is also affected by the randomness of the events in the surroundings, most of them beyond our control. And since most outcomes involve a substantial contribution of those random events, it's only wise that we have a certain incentive to keep trying again and not get disheartened. For all that you can do is try.

And since the definition of success and failure will keep changing as you move forward, its inherent dynamic nature can get the better of you. In any way, they remain to be the two sides of the same coin that you ultimately will have to flip at many stages of your life, and whatever side it lands on, life has to go on and with it the efforts to have that next flip fall in our favour.

And the only way is to accept the possibility of failure as taking a calculated risk of losing your time, effort and investments, in pursuit of meaningful achievements.

As they say, 'He has achieved success who has lived well, laughed often, and loved much.'

Other than that, after a certain point, all of what you consider success and failure would not matter at all.

Sometimes, failing a lot in life and not being regretful about not trying what you always wanted to be is also what makes people happy, for they made their best possible effort at it.

And to add to it, when you look back at your life if you have been able to spend time with your loved ones, have fewer regrets and more beautiful memories, have been able to maintain good health while managing your responsibilities, and were able to spend time on something that you really liked and felt happy doing—all of it does seem like a successful and a beautiful life.

Since that goal is exactly like life, it's all about the process and the journey, not just the destination. It's the process that defines whether we reach that ultimate goal or not.

Whichever way we choose to see it, it's about not living with the "what ifs" and "what you could not" but savouring all of what you could and did.

And to everyone's surprise, while still being a failure to everyone else by their definitions, you could still choose to be YOUR successful and YOUR happy version of YOU.

* * *

8
Social Media

Ever looked up from your phone's screen and wondered where the last hour or two has gone while staring at it?

Or noticed how you can't help picking that device up again and again for no apparent reason throughout the day? It's easy to lose track of time while doing that. With one in every hand and their reach increasing every day, it's taking over our lives ever so easily.

And to add to it, most of us have become addicted to staying connected, with which we are inadvertently exposed to information streams in various forms.

We do know that the addiction is doing harm to us and depriving us of real opportunities for interaction but many a times we act like zombies, using our phones without knowing why, bringing them out as a reflex action and losing ourselves in it for hours, apparently doing nothing at all.

It allows us to remain in a parallel world where we can easily look into other people's lives and also display the highlights of our lives probably because we believe it to be the new formula for social acceptance and validation. The more likes we get on a picture of our holiday, the more we tend to want on our next, as a sign of our social acceptance and popularity among a large list of friends. This also serves one more purpose, to show the world that we are having a good time as well, and sometimes better than theirs.

Many times, we choose to be immersed in a smartphone rather than a meaningful interaction with the family and friends and taking countless pictures and selfies every day, which eventually get lost in the sea of pictures anyway.

The research shows that the average attention span of a person addicted to smartphones has less than halved and that ratio is even less when you have the device in your vicinity. If you spend considerable time on the internet, you will agree with it since you would've already noticed having difficulty focusing on tasks at hand without getting distracted.

More than 90% of information we consume daily is of no use to us. Not now, and most of it not even in the future.

The sources include the internet, social media, and messaging apps, and also to some extent, all the interactions we have with real people. Many times, we turn our phones on in between an important task and end up stuck to it for hours and hours without doing anything at all, endlessly scrolling through mindless information and data.

Hundreds of WhatsApp and Telegram groups we are a part of keep buzzing out notifications with a constant stream of trivial information playing with our minds.

Just to put things in perspective, the amount of data or information generated and consumed on the internet has increased exponentially. Earlier, it was the organisations that did the most of it, but since the last few years, every single one of us with a smartphone or an internet connection is adding to it every minute.

There is an unlimited amount of data in the form of text, video, and audio available for us to access, and it keeps us continuously scrolling through related content when we search for something that interests us.

And most of the time, the continuous exposure to all of it gets overwhelming to an extent that it leaves us exhausted and anxious.

These platforms crave our continuous attention and presence on the platform, but how do we curate the useful information from the redundant ones? Or even know that the content we are looking at isn't misinformation in its present form without any verifying mechanisms.

What to believe and what not to, or even how to differentiate true knowledge from fake narratives. For in the age, we are in, we must always take everything on the internet with a pinch of salt.

More than the information, it's turning into a time where fake news and misinformation have become a bigger problem for society and vulnerable individuals. Especially with the use of AI and Deepfakes, it's becoming increasingly difficult to identify the real from fake.

A lot of people fall for it and forward it without giving it a second thought since it looks convincing to people with confirmation bias. There are also fake social media accounts, and bots that help spread propaganda, fake information, and help it go viral. Anyone can claim to be an expert on a random subject and upload whatever and whenever they deem fit, using clickbait's to gain our attention and presence.

Our attention is being sold; the more time you spend on these platforms, the more opportunities there are for them to show you advertisements and sponsored content. The attention and the data of people has become the most important commodity, and for the coming generations, it can include but is certainly not limited to your likes, dislikes, places visited, credit history, and your whereabouts at a certain moment.

The internet and the social media platforms are built to be addictive, but believing anything you see on it as the hard truth and spending so much time staring at the screens can cause damage beyond repair.

The Data

The current generation has no qualms about sharing the details of their personal lives, pictures, and events on the internet and believes in being social and share everything with a whole lot more than their close circle of friends. The more friends on social networks, the more they are considered famous, relevant or wanted. The more likes received on social media posts, the more it makes them feel good and accepted.

The medium has the good, the bad, and the ugly based on how you choose to use it and react to it. It's also the source of constant engagements for the lonely and a business tool for many.

Though the advent of social media facilitates a revolution allowing us to keep in touch with a host of people from our lives we would've lost touch with otherwise, it also allows businesses to flourish globally and provides them a level playing field by allowing them to reach out to people for a fraction of the cost or none at all.

But gradually, it's taking a form that we couldn't have imagined when all of it started. An addiction like no other the world has seen, wherein there is no age and time limit to its use, entirely legal and available to everyone, and yes, it's slowly getting more addictive.

In a way, addictions like gambling and social media are quite similar since both of these activities cause the same response in the brain to keep you hooked and wanting to go back again and again. It's just that you may lose your money in the first and a whole lot of your time in the second.

If you are addicted, you are not alone. And if it can make you feel a bit better, you are not at fault. This is how the human brain functions, and you cannot do a thing about it. Since most of these social media apps remain free, your all-day attention is the fee you pay to them.

Social media companies even hire attention engineers and experts to try and use human psychology to keep you glued to social media and information apps all day and make them as addictive as possible.

It's a vicious cycle of unlimited content, and the more time you spend on these apps, the more content is consumed, shared or generated.

Scrolling through social media can be very stimulating, almost to an extent that you are unable to withdraw even when you want to. It's almost as if we are infected by some disease that forces us to go back to it again and again.

It's only when you get to see the measure of time spent on it in any of the Screentime apps on your phone that you realise the gravity of the situation and the addiction.

The current normal screen time of adults has reached an average of 6-8 hours a day, and for the time we are off that screen, we spend it with thoughts of going back to it for different reasons. The case with most of us, if not everyone.

Scary already, isn't it?

It's affecting your life a lot more than you realise, but how do we decide how much is too much, and more than that, how do we stop if it's a red flag?

Also, to put things into perspective, it's only been a few years since our generation has had the full-fledged access to smartphones, and it's already causing havoc. Imagine the next generation, namely the Alphas and the Betas, in which everyone has had access to technology of this magnitude since day one, an entire generation that has not seen or experienced the times before technology took over, what could it lead to??

Surrounded all day by tech is going to be their 'normal' state of being since birth, and that's exactly why it's even going to get worse.

Comparison

But why exactly does the device or the apps have that much of our attention all day long?

Under any given conditions, when we are happy, sad, or tired, it's the smartphone and social media that we turn to.

The answer lies in the word 'Comparison' and the continuous need to validate ourselves and stay relevant based on that.

It's the comparison based on the social media feeds of others that makes us believe that others have a better life than what we have, look and dress better than we do, have more likes and shares on their posts which in turn make them more popular than us.

You can be having a good day, and when you open your apps, you see everyone having a better time, which instantly robs you of your present where you suddenly start to want to be somewhere else, doing something better, and sometimes be with someone else as well to feel better.

We all want social approval and also to know what people think of us. And that dopamine release with the appreciation and approvals online does make you want more of it often.

But comparison in its very state is a source of stress, more so when it's on social media because that's not the real life of someone we are comparing ourselves to, but rather the highlights of someone's life to our everyday real life and for the same reason it has become important to know what goes behind the scenes and the reel vs reality of the matter.

Hours of posing and editing for that everyday pic, a lot of scripting and practise for that random video, and multiple clicks for that perfect photo are sometimes all that's done to show us that one perfect moment of someone's life.

No one can look good all the time, have fun, or be in an ecstatic mood all the while. The relationships may not be so perfect as they are made to appear, and that one picture posted may be the best one among the hundreds clicked. People modify their pictures to appear better looking, curate their best photos to look their best on Instagram. Added with effects and filters, sometimes the posts do make the life of others look almost perfect.

All of it does take a toll on our mental health. When stress shows up, we are not turning to a person; we are turning to social media again most of the time, to scroll through the new information that's been uploaded while we were feeling miserable.

Also, all of it ends up distorting our idea of reality. The perfect looks, how a romantic relationship should pan out, and then comparing all of it to our reality. And also, our perceptions of how things are supposed to be when they are not. For people who believe everything they see on the internet, the unrealistic standards are affecting their lives and relationships big time.

No one shows their relationship troubles, when they are being out of perfect shape or feeling bloated, or not looking their best, their struggles with mindset and temperament, and especially their imperfections on these social platforms.

However, all of these are unavoidable parts of our lives and will occur regardless of whatever we do to avoid them.

The best of something or someone or the perceived excellence that you see may not always be attainable in real life for most owing to different reasons and sometimes it may even not be the truth as it is shown to be.

And it sets up a lot of expectations about how our lives should be, when all we should be doing is taking things as they happen and dealing with them on their own merit, instead of comparing ourselves, people, and experiences

And when our expectations don't meet our reality, we start to suffer.

Studies have linked excessive use of social media and the internet to anxiety, sleep deprivation, loss of focus, and impatience. Despite providing access to an infinite number of friends on the platform, it often leaves individuals feeling lonely.

We start spending more time on it, preferring it more to the real conversations. We get angry at small possibilities of discomfort and make impulsive decisions just because we want to go back to the phones quickly, which in turn starts affecting the real relationships.

Showing the world certain aspects of the so-called happening life has become a norm, but it should not be associated with the overall well-being of a person. It's like creating a fake narrative of your life to sell to your friend list while, in reality, one continues to be in misery.

It's like sending an ecstatic smiley on WhatsApp in reply to something when it doesn't even make you smile in real life.

When you consistently keep your mind engaged by hopping from one app to another, it becomes accustomed to the constant influx of information. So, when you finally set the phone aside, your mind starts craving more stimulation. If the device is within reach, the urge to pick it up again becomes so strong that eventually, you feel compelled to do so.

There is no dearth of addictive apps that entice the human brain to keep clicking on it as there may be something exciting or important that should not be missed.

When one is done tweeting, they take the time to scroll through Facebook and Instagram posts and reels, check WhatsApp and Snapchat for any new messages and status updates, keep clicking selfies on various photo apps, applying filters to look their best, and tagging people, posting them on various platforms to fetch more likes. Once we are done with the last app on our phone, the first one we used an hour back is ready with new and exciting data that makes us go through the whole same cycle again and again.

There is a constant inflow of information on the internet, and we are not made to handle this much barrage of information continuously, let alone process and retain it. That's why we keep forgetting things and struggle to remember important information since there is so much going on inside our mind, and since it could only process a fraction of it at a time. We could be in the midst of something urgent and important, but as the information flow starts, the brain gets clouded and confused, and suddenly we start to lose the plot.

Many times, you might find yourself engaged in something important or enjoying playful moments with your family, yet not fully present in the moment, having the persistent urge to return to your device and apps driven by fear of missing out. This state of absent-minded presence is almost akin to not being fully there and savouring the moments. If these moments slip away, they may never return.

Sometimes we spend long hours on the shopping websites, scrolling through endless options, adding them to our carts, and looking for the best deals. How much of it do we actually need, and how much of it do we actually end up buying? And even if we do, how much of it turns out to be a useful choice?

The easier access to information and media opens the door to a lot that's unwanted. The effect of smartphones can be easily seen on child psychology and development. For children, human interactions are the primary source of learning and growth in which they build ideas based on what's happening around them. The brains are being rewired, and if they are allowed to use gadgets extensively, they start facing difficulty focusing even on simple tasks and remain absent-minded with so much data and information to make sense of at any single moment.

They replicate the behaviour they are able to see in their favourite cartoon characters, which is sometimes violent and indecent, also being exposed to a lot of information impassively before the requisite time of life, including sex and violence.

Going to a restaurant, most families on the table are found looking at their mobile phones instead of talking to each other, and it's visible to the kids. They learn and replicate what they see, and obviously, they won't see any wrong in what their family is doing. You can only imagine the amount of time your kid sees you looking at your phone, let alone the actual amount of time you spend on it. These challenges invariably have a negative impact on relationships, and if left unaddressed, they can persist indefinitely, potentially affecting individuals and their connections for a lifetime.

Social media plays with your productivity in different ways. Since most social media apps are free to use, all they want is our undivided and continuous attention as remuneration for it, and that remains to be a very big cost to pay. Moreover, excessive social media usage often leads to various forms of anxiety, prompting individuals to seek refuge in it rather than addressing real-world situations.

Do you remember when the last time was that you were sitting doing nothing or reading a newspaper or a book without going through smartphone app notifications?

And for that matter, when was the last time you had lost track of time while spending time with your loved ones without a smartphone around?

It's very much possible that instead of your online time causing depression, the depression is causing more time to be spent online. It's like keeping a lot of tabs on a computer web browser and compulsively checking each one of them every few hours or minutes.

It's the unpredictability of the media that keeps us coming back to it. The mind gets a reward in the form of new and exciting information when we push that refresh button on the endless feed or click on that app when there is a notification. The brain has a way of judging what's worth doing again, irrespective of it being productive or not.

You can have a panic attack even if you forget to carry your mobile phone with you when you step out for extended periods of time, and you will have a restless time until you get it back and see what you missed out on.

Smartphone apps also take advantage of our inherent social anxieties, which also involve the fear of missing out (FOMO), making us believe that we need to receive the information and reciprocate it as soon as possible.

Also, for the reason that the smartphone has so much personal data on it, that you do not want to have the slightest chance to allow someone to snoop on it, you want to keep it with you all the time.

How many times have you refused to play with your kids and handed over a tablet or another phone to them to not disturb you because you were busy on social media?

A lot of us check the WhatsApp messages and emails in the middle of the night and also the first thing in the morning, carrying the phone in meeting halls and dinners with close friends and remaining glued to the screen, it's because we have become addicted and have given in to the temptations of the fake in lieu of your relationships.

Too much of tech can leave you anxious and exhausted since, for most of us, the use of it has become out of balance. The truth is that it has become almost impossible to draw fair usage lines until we come forward and accept that it's time.

It's definitely something to worry about if not having access to your phone for some time is making you anxious, you sleep late because of it, and the first thing you do is pick up your phone in the morning, and your conversations and relationships are being affected due to the brain drain.

Although all of that is mentioned here does paint social media as evil which isn't always entirely true. It has given a host of people opportunities that they couldn't even think of before, the platforms have become the voice for the weak and source of knowledge for the uninformed and there hasn't been a time when the common people had so much they could learn and execute with the help of the internet and social media for free. It's the excessive use of it and the ways it is been exploited that's more of a worry than its inherent nature.

Ours and the next generation remains to be an instant gratification generation, the swipe left, swipe right ones. We don't like to wait long for anything, not for the food, not the cab, not even for relationships to run their course. We have almost begun to desire things at the speed of thought.

The instant availability of everything is making us impatient to the point where we no longer want to give the necessary time to the aspects of life that inherently require a long time to develop, ultimately resulting in a fulfilling life.

But however, you choose to look at it, everything meaningful in life takes time and effort and happens more often in the real world and not in the confines of our mobile screens. The deeper connections, relationships, and beliefs take time to develop with their own ups and downs and there is no app for that.

Once in a while, it becomes important for us to disconnect from the chaos to connect and ponder over things that have been craving our attention or finish the tasks that have been pending for the want of undivided attention for a long time.

The list is long and tiring, and the solution is easy. It's just that you will have to admit and agree to the problem and know what's important and what's not and be brave enough to decide and limit the use of it and give time to real relations to nurture them for a lasting and fulfilling experience.

Yes, you can appear to be happy on social media without doing all of it, just making faces, editing pics, and pretending to be happy. But it depends on you whether you want to just look happy to others or rather feel it for yourself.

The window of relevance on social media has shrunk so much that the content you post hardly makes a difference anymore. If you think otherwise, take a break from posting on these platforms for a month, and you'll see that hardly anyone cares as much as you thought they would.

Contrary to the popular opinion that multitasking is advantageous, the human mind, though having unlimited capabilities, does better when devoted to only one task at a time where complete focus on that task is involved.

In our desire for continuous updates and data to satisfy our craving minds, we've forgotten to press the pause button and spend some time doing nothing at all. We've lost the art of getting bored without reaching for our phones to check for new updates, or our laptops to browse emails or social media for redundant information or entertainment.

To walk with our heads up, not listening to tracks but looking around and noticing things, to actually stop and talk to random people once in a while and enjoy some time by just being completely in the moment and not being distracted by notifications.

Maybe we really need to go back to the dumb phone once in a while to feel smart again or be less anxious, for that matter.

It's time we get a life outside of that phone or even leave it behind sometimes to see how this affects us.

And also, it's time for us to realise that sometimes we can actually have a good time without constantly clicking pictures and making videos to post on the internet, just to show others that we are having a good time.

Stop Phubbing the real relationships, break free from FOMO and avoid being a Smombie.

That's all we can strive for.

✳ ✳ ✳

9
Generations

Education begins early these days, all aspects of it. The very moment kids get access to the internet and social media.

We could notice young kids talking a lot of sense and logic sometimes. How did they grow smarter? Is there something different with the current generation? Probably not, since it has more to do with the abundant information they can access and are exposed to all day long.

The conventional education system doesn't add value to the early age potential and learning capacity the next generation holds. There are streams and careers which require us to devote a number of years to study before one can become a professional at something and also make money out of it. But that path isn't the only one available and applicable now.

Kids today, and even their parents, don't want them to wait 15-20 years to become an expert at something and then start their careers. Instead, they prefer going through various possibilities through the internet, social media, learning new theories and systems.

Also, they don't want to do just one thing and believe that they can start learning and execute a lot of things now while also pursuing conventional career paths which will obviously take a lot of time but still doesn't guarantee any success.

The human brain always had this potential to learn a whole lot at the early stages of life, and the current system's pace of providing education and the relevance of it has always been a shortcoming of it.

You often see young kids and their parents inclined to expose them to learning early, as well as to a variety of other activities, so they can start exploring their passions and options. And similar to education, with the right opportunities, progress has begun to come early as well.

Also, in the last few decades, other than the regular subjects, other streams of interest have also come up as major career options, be it public speaking performances, editing videos for various platforms for creators on YouTube and Instagram, a career in music and sports, learning about all of which can begin from the outset and not when you start to search for an alternate one when the conventional ones don't work out for them.

You could be a doctor and a musician, a lawyer and a public speaker, or an entrepreneur while pursuing many other interests. And while doing all of this, the art of communication and public speaking skills remain to be the most important of the coming times.

Yes, a lot of famous people in the world have been introverts, and public interactions haven't been their best foot forward, but the times have changed, and it's become imperative to speak and convey what you feel and what you are good at must find its way to the masses or else it can get lost in the narratives and chaos of the world, and a direct conversation remains by far the best way to communicate with those who want to listen to your story.

The psychology of money remains equally important in the similar manner, for when the kids start to make it, they must know the value of it for them and everyone else and the ways to use it for personal and professional growth.

There are a lot of chaotic situations and people the young will have to deal with when they grow up, sometimes even with some of them they wouldn't want to. But that's how it is, there will be teams they will have to be flexible to be a part of, be patient in the chaos, stay sane during the altercations, listen more to learn more, resolve conflicts, and sometimes be okay with the unresolved ones.

Learning all of it took a lifetime for the previous generation but since exposure to life situations, career choices, relationships are happening early for the kids now, it's only fair that we teach them the coping mechanisms early as well.

If we still expect them to pursue a certain conventional career, it's always okay to let them explore more on the side.

Their chosen paths may not make much sense at that time to the seniors, but it may very well prove to be much better than what we think would be better for them. And that's why letting them pursue their interests, learn with hit and trial is the best possible thing that parents could do for them

Let's talk about the instant gratification generation, The Z.

A generation which grew up using technology in abundance. Smartphones, tablets, computer systems, electronic gadgets, and whatnot since their early days.

The Gen Z are smart, intelligent, demanding, impatient, and a no-compromise generation. They seem to know everything, or at least they think they do.

Incredibly ambitious, they want everything and want it instantly. No more waiting in lines, no more buffering videos, and no more slow progress – they want everything ultra-fast. They have no patience for uninformed viewpoints and below-par talks.

They spend a lot of time on social media and contribute to a major chunk of its content. Be it useful news alerts on Twitter or redundant pics of food items on their table, they are everywhere. They manage to get noticed everywhere for the spark they always carry along.

They believe in the importance of education and behaviour. They know their rights and have a lot of tools at their disposal to voice their dissent if they need to. For them, the definition of success is not just accumulating wealth; they want to use their money and not just save it for future generations.

But why do millennials, a generation that attained adulthood in the early 21ˢᵗ century, find them reckless? Probably because of the difference in priorities, compliances, and thought processes.

If the Gen Z are asked about millennials viewpoints, they may not agree with many things the previous generation follows and does. The difference in beliefs and practices is obvious and expected.

Though throughout the history, people have initially believed that forthcoming generations are not as hardworking as they should be, are entitled and selfish, and don't behave as per the standards and benchmarks set by the current ones, the Gen Z introduces a new dimension to this trend, as they seem to be driven by a completely different force – technology.

The reliance of people in this generation on technology has become so evident and enormous that there isn't a day in our lives without spending a considerable amount of time glued to screens at the cost of regular and normal interactions with people around.

Old parenting skills don't apply anymore. The learning now doesn't involve what the parents choose to teach but rather what the kids want to learn and listen.

The choice of subjects that the internet and social media have given them is staggering, and it's more of Google and Instagram that will have a say in how their lives shape up than their parents.

This will keep changing with more exposure to information and fascination with possibilities. There is only a certain time until when you can teach a kid what to do, what is right and wrong, and expect them to take your word for it. After that, whatever they are told, they will certainly find contradictory information on all the platforms. The hammering of which may convince them that what was taught to them all along was just to keep them in line.

Apart from that, how we can really make them believe in something is only by setting the example right, by doing what we preach and that being visible to them. That alone remains a way to make them believe more in our side of the story than all else where they are being told otherwise.

But what exactly does being a good kid mean? Is it not causing chaos and not disagreeing with the parents or not doing something when they are told not to? For the parents of this generation, it seems to be that the kids figure out things on their own and not trouble them about it and let them do their own things at peace.

Kids develop the need for personal space and boundaries of discussion early now and tend to want their privacy, sometimes for reasons not to the liking of the parents. As they grow up, they want to make their own decisions based on what they think may turn out to be the best way for them.

But if there is a definition of a good kid for you, there must be one of a good parent as well.

Some people still believe that children are a way to carry forward their legacy and expect them to do things and behave a certain way and follow traditions that the family has been following for generations.

For some parents, they are the source of all happiness, and it becomes their life's goal to provide them with the best possible of everything they could. Help them with everything and fight for them even at the sign of slight discomfort to them.

People invest all their finances and emotional capital into raising the children, and when it starts to not turn out the way they expect it to, it leads to dissatisfactions and distances, sometimes lasting forever.

But why give them all that baggage to begin with in the first place, which can leave them dissatisfied all their lives, for all they could not achieve, rather than being content and happy for what they could.

Expectations

Expectations, sometimes to the extent of being unrealistic, are most of the times the source of all disappointments for all parties involved.

From the perspective of a Guardian, we will have to understand that lesser the expectations, the fewer the chances that we will be disappointed. Though expecting and conveying some of the probable and reasonable things is necessary, for it informs the person of the dedication and responsible actions expected.

From the perspective of that of the Young, it's important to know that they will have a lot of obvious expectations from the parents since they are the ones, they rely on for everything.

But since, in most cases, the expected and the reality are much different and since there are so many of expectations at a time, it's never possible for anyone to deliver on all the parameters.

And sometimes people are attached too much to the expected outcomes that all else other than that appears much less interesting and fruitful to them. Also, that the people close to us, especially the parents, are bad at estimating the things that will make us happy and rather look at it from their viewpoint to come to not-so-wise conclusions, for they know little about our actual mindset for a fulfilling career and life.

Still, probably with more conventional wisdom and experience, we can agree that they may know more about life and the priorities and challenges the young and naïve will face at the later stages of life.

Similar is the case with comparison, and it could also result in a stark contrast effect when done wrong. The theory suggests the relativity of comparison and states that when you look at something or someone by making a benchmark for what they should be doing or should've achieved by comparing them to other people and their success stories, the difference appears much stark than it actually is. You must also know that life and its treatment are different for everyone, and the pace at which it happens to us is also variable for different individuals.

Yes, it's good to make plans for a loved one and have a vision for them of how their careers should play out and the paths they should take and the choices they should make, which will aid them in achieving those perceived results but in this generation, doing all of it only seems feasible until they are not wise enough to decide for themselves.

Yes, what parents can teach them is to be more responsible in their major decisions as the results of it affects relationships, finances, and ultimately their future. But that's the aspect of what we can teach them the importance of and not the actual decisions that they need to make.

But beyond wanting the best for your child for emotional reasons and guiding them, it's also crucial to recognize the right time to let go of some responsibilities and allow them to handle things on their own.

Decisions, right or wrong, when taken, only make one wiser. Unless we free the kids to decide, they won't be able to make their own decisions and make mistakes, for everyone must make their fair share of mistakes for it to teach them the ways of life, how it works and more of how it doesn't.

If they are not allowed to do that, how can we expect them to begin the learning curve of their responsibilities and life?

But there is also one more problem with expectations and comparisons. All of it is based on the right and wrong definitions and processes and rules of the past. One where it doesn't take into account what the person from whom something is being expected thinks of it and second that it becomes the root of all the heartburn for both sides.

The way the current and next generations are being raised seems to hold the answers to all these issues. The parents started having fewer children for various reasons, including strained finances and the incremental cost of raising a child, impending future expenses and along with all of it, maintaining a decent lifestyle for themselves. And since they wanted the best for their child, such would not be possible with a bunch of kids to be raised and only limited resources and time available to do that.

And since they had only a few children, they were more loved and cared for, kept away from any negative feedback for it should not damage their self-esteem. They were told that they are special and could do and achieve anything they want to, provided with all the material possessions and facilities that their parents could not have access to and, in turn, didn't want to deny their children of those.

The more ambitious the parents grew, the more time they wanted for their work, and less time they began to devote to their kids. Instead, they started covering the shortcomings by showering possessions and gifts at them. Children from a very early age are given mobile phones and tablets so that they don't disturb their parents. Parents are allowing smartphones or tablets to play nanny to their kids, forgetting that they are denying the children the most important thing they deserve: their parents' time and undivided attention.

This generation has a lot more to offer than the previous can fathom and make sense of. But it's especially in this one that the young ones of the affluent are raised, being protected from anything remotely uncomfortable, with the feeling of being the special ones. They are told that they are to achieve great things in life, to make an impact on society, and have the potential to bring about a change for the better.

While their importance for the family is significant, it doesn't carry forward to the real world. When they are thrust into normal life, their dreams suddenly take a backseat when they realise that they cannot have everything just because they want to and were told that they can.

Not all follow the rules they were told they should, and they aren't the best at what they do. Everything they try to do has more hurdles than support systems. In total, life isn't always fair, not even to the most deserving sometimes.

They cannot make an impact just because their parents told them that they are capable of doing so. Their whole world comes crashing down.

Are we actually making life harder for children by not being strict with them now, or are we potentially setting them up for a difficult life by shielding them from failure or disappointment and not allowing them to navigate through challenges and situations on their own?

In a way, which means they will always remain dependent on someone to figure out the solutions for them. Should we stop explaining to them that the only way they are considered successful is if they find that place on the winner's podium.

Or should we suppress the culture of false confidence that we have developed for protecting our children so that they don't have to deal with disappointments early in their lives, giving in to everything they wish for so that they don't feel sad about it?

They will have to face that eventually and be distraught at the real feeling of it, which would be exponentially more compared to if they have had a taste of it early in their life.

How to handle failure is the most important skill that we can teach anyone, for there will be more than enough of those on a daily basis, and the random emotions attached to that can make-or-break the mindset for all things in life.

Explaining failure as a positive outcome for future preparation and not getting disheartened by it, informing them of the value of effort and the involvement of random occurrences in the result, may just make them feel better and be ready to try again when it's time, with more preparation and less worry about the reaction of people when they fail and of the knowledge that if they want to get on that podium, they will have to keep trying.

Encouraging effort can be more useful than protecting one from anything and everything, even if it results in failure, since that exposure makes us learn new dimensions about various aspects of life.

Generation Gap

It's not them or us; it's what we believe in.

And it may not always be possible and wise to fill that gap or even try to do that, for it may even end up widening it.

The lessons learned since childhood and the observations made in the surrounding environment and so deeply ingrained in our minds that it's not easy to change a belief at the outset and takes a lot of effort and time to believe otherwise.

But with changing times and different ways of it, it has become important to be in line with modern-day traditions or else be disappointed with looking at the changing behaviour and mannerisms of loved ones.

Still, some of us choose to remain conservative and follow the same traditions, which in a way is fruitful and responsible for some of our important traditions to still be relevant and practised. The balance is though very necessary as the next generation wants freedom from the redundant and considers a lot of practices and compulsions from the past as baggage and not useful enough.

When it's about the career and one wants to choose what they want to pursue, the presence of a generation gap becomes more evident. Even today, if the parents hold a certain high regard for a profession, which as per them is more respectful and monetarily rewarding, they will push their children to become a part of it and have preconceived notions about how the child must represent and carry forward their legacy. Some don't want girls to study much and prefer them to be homemakers at best. They are less respectful of their demands and choices compared to the male child, let alone talk about them making a career out of things they are passionate about.

One must acknowledge that, in these times, careers in sports, entertainment, and the arts have also emerged as viable options for the younger generation. Sometimes, when parents just want their children becoming doctors or engineers, they are ignoring the scope of growth and prosperity in these areas of vocation.

There are numerous examples where parents haven't been supportive, yet the children, despite this lack of support, have achieved significant success, ultimately making their parents proud. The relationships that the kids have chosen to have turned out to be more successful than the ones chosen by the wise ones. The friends disapproved of and have turned out to be more helpful than the relatives considered close.

You can choose to be a parent who enjoys drinks with the young and discuss variety over it, including the harms of excess of it, or one who disapproves and prohibits it since it's bad for them and considered wrong by society, while they still do it in your absence anyway.

No one knows everything and can always be right, but if a person seems to have the right intent and knows how to take calculated risks, they should be given enough chances to wholeheartedly pursue the career they want to choose, the relationships they want to get into, and let destiny play its part.

Is the situation really that bad that the boomers have made it out to be? And is the current generation really distracted from the priorities of life?

Every generation has had its distractions in the form of new inventions and discoveries, but none like this one. The use of technology has easily surpassed the interest in actual and detailed human interactions which are necessary to build emotional bonds.

The generation has everything going for it—the technology, the opportunities, the freedom of choice and expression, access to resources and information. But sometimes it feels like there is too much of everything available to them.

Too much choice, too much assurance, too much flexibility, and too much of anything creates chaos and indecision.

The world has started changing at a much faster pace, and the speed of it will only increase with the exponential speed of advances in technology and science being made. The thoughts and processes we have now and want to teach others may not hold water for much longer.

And we must already know that there is no point in teaching the kids the ways of the world other than only a few that we consider really important in all situations.

On a broader note, in the future, all that children will ask for and all we will be able to offer is financial support and emotional backing when they reach out for it. And believe it or not, they will have a difficult time navigating through life as the world has become chaotic in its very nature.

The next gen will have to learn to flourish in the chaos and also know how to keep away from it when it's time.

But the thing with chaos is sometimes a lot of it is unavoidable, and with it comes a lot of information and situations that we have to deal with and make sense of.

One may know a lot of things but doesn't know what to believe and move forward with. One may want to do a lot of things but cannot figure out how to. Everyone realises the importance of time but doesn't know how to use it wisely or for the better.

Generation Z, the first native digital generation may seem reckless to the millennials, always looking for an easier way out, not heeding to traditions and conventional rules of the society but they remain to be a bright lot.

Not to forget that the oldest of them is still only 28 implying they haven't yet lived their wiser years to have the level of maturity the millennials expect them to.

And it's important to give them time before judging them since eventually like every other generation, they will also figure everything out when its time.

And when its time, they will also understand and figure out why the millennials, The x and the boomers thought of them that way.

When it's time for them to deal with the generation alpha and the beta, they will have that respect and admiration for all that we did and were able to manage, that we demand from them now.

Yes, a lot of them are entitled brats but when life will happen to them like everyone else, they will be back on track and may be do much better than what we wanted them to at the first place.

Only things we could and should want them to know could be the importance of relationships, life skills and Value of Order and Discipline in Life. To tell them to not fall for anything and everything they are told and see on the internet and also in the real world.

That not all the problems will have solutions and not all people will end up liking them for what they do and who they are.

And we must also teach them the power of belief and purpose, as these elements shape who we become and how we spend our lives far more than our ambitions alone.

And how to not wait to achieve that goal to be happy in life.

And that 'There is no secret Ingredient' of how life shapes up.

It's important to tell them that now since after a while, It would just be them, and probably a bit of Us in them that we would have left behind when we are gone.

10

Fitness

We are what we eat …and what we don't.
And how we move adds a whole lot to that.

The idea is simple: if you are not happy about something, make efforts to change it. Conscious choices in nutrition, adequate water intake, a regular exercise routine, sufficient deep sleep, and taking care of your mental health, along with proper knowledge of what suits your body and what doesn't, can help you achieve most of what you intend. It's all common knowledge and sounds easy, but why do we find it difficult to execute?

Is it the lack of discipline or just the craving for instant rewards in the form of taste or comfort?

People do like to read and talk about every aspect of it, but when it comes to execution, it's a tough nut to crack for most. Since it involves a process that requires a lot of discipline and consistent efforts most people give up. Like everything else we strive for, committing to this process also requires a focused understanding of the 'why' behind it.

Also what is not easy is the mental aspect of it. The mindset, the emotions, the chaos in the mind, and the discipline and effort needed to keep the mind clear of distractions and calm amidst the chaos can sometimes prove to be an impossible task given the circumstances of one's life

Mental health includes our emotional, behavioural, and psychological well-being but is often overlooked as an important aspect of your overall fitness. It's also affects how people feel, think, behave, and respond to situations.

One of the worst things about mental illness is how it affects your life, from even the most mundane things on a daily basis to the most important ones. Your mental state governs your day and decides how you feel about your work, relations, and all other aspects of life. It was an alien subject a decade ago, but now the problem and discussions about it are raging worldwide among people of all ages.

But why is the mental health scenario much different from the physical aspect of it?

Mostly because it's easy to derive standard procedures and knowledge for a good state of physical being but with the mind it's a different setup for each individual. There could be different reasons and experiences that cause a certain state of mind and in turn the problems with it.

Also, a scenario where people are not able to relate to or understand the aspects of it, because the reasons behind it for some people may sound absolutely redundant and trivial to the others.

Persistent negative thoughts, feelings of emptiness, and a sense of hopelessness, sometimes without any apparent reason, can cause the mind to spiral, making it difficult to figure out the reasons and solutions for those.

It's an explosive situation and the mental health crisis looks like an impending Global pandemic of the next few decades.

The cause of anxiety and depression could be anything from wanting or doing much more than we already are, some trauma from the past, or not being able to handle the loss of someone dear or losing motivation for life under stressful circumstances or something as simple as comparisons or a life choice that you made and are still facing the heat for.

Strangely enough, for some people not having a problem also becomes a part of the problem. The human tendency is to get bored with the normal and aspire to achieve or do something different and for the very reason the absolutely normal life situations can also cause a state of mental dissatisfaction.

The mind behaves in an unpredictable manner when there is a lot of information and situations being continuously fed to it, since there cannot be an overflow, it starts to churn out unrelatable emotions with random occurrences of it. The information overload forms a major chunk of the reason behind the random swings in thoughts and emotions in any case.

You could be happy at one and sad at the next moment. Calm at one and Angry at another instance. And it gets difficult to make logic of any of it.

How do you manage to get out of a situation you cannot figure out the reason for in the first place? Or what if the reason is something you cannot do anything about?

Though the trigger can be different for everyone, in most cases, the fluctuations can be reduced if not completely treated by adopting to a disciplined life scenario where in when you have your day planned and know what is to be done at what time, your mind is less anxious as it knows what's coming, what situations to expect and its responses to them.

For many of us, identifying the reasons, doing something about it or making peace with it, trying to always have something to look forward to, finding a like-minded community, finding a purpose and a routine may prove to be the best possible solution to navigate out of the spiral.

Some individuals opt for substance abuse to alleviate present discomfort, but this often ends up increasing the intensity of their struggles when the effects wear off.

A lot of people affected by mental health issues keep a brave face and not let the people know about it, for sometimes it's difficult to be considered weak and vulnerable They keep themselves merged in random tasks all day to prevent the availability of time for them to again have that persistent sadness trouble them. But it's important to discuss it with the close ones rather than keep it to self and continue suffering.

The struggles can be small or big, but they are a reality and a lot of us are increasingly becoming exposed to it if not already affected by the wayward emotions already. And it's important to seek help when the situation arises, as it's imperative to not let it go deep and attend to it when it begins.

And there is no age where it can start affecting you …

Food.

Yes, we are what we eat.

And by the quantity of it as well.

The choice of food has to also be complemented by the portion size. Even if something is healthy and nutritional, we still cannot eat the same thing in unlimited quantities every time, since the body needs a variety of nutrients.

It's the dosage of anything that differentiates it from being a poison or a remedy and no food is inherently evil in its purest form to being with. Even the best of foods can prove to be dangerous when consumed in excessive quantities.

You must remain in a calorie deficit if you are looking to lose weight and in a surplus if you want to gain it. When you decide to do this through a combination of food and exercise, you have to monitor the nutritional profile closely to ensure that the weight you are gaining is more in the form of muscle and that which is being lost is in the form of fat.

When you lose weight without proper exercise and nutrition then along with the unwanted fat you lose muscle as well which is a deterrent to keeping you fit in the long-term. The aim should be to lose the undesired fat and build more muscle in place of it.

Also remember that healthy fat loss methods take time and whatever stage your body is in right now is a result of a long-term habits and process and trying to reverse that with a short-term change would do more damage than good.

When you plan to remain in a caloric surplus or deficit, make sure you first remove the empty calories and foods that are devoid of any nutrition.

But how do we identify what is good and bad? Who do we listen to?

Diets like vegan, keto, paleo, and others are almost impossible to follow. Intermittent fasting windows aren't for everyone. Experts have different views on which foods they consider harmful, and there is no universally similar effect of one food on all bodies.

Some ask you to stay vegetarian, while others prefer non-vegetarian diets. Some may advocate consuming milk and eggs, while others ask you to reject these completely due to their perceived long-term harmful effects. Additionally, some diets emphasize the importance of whole grains, while others suggest eliminating them altogether. There are those who recommend high-fat, low-carb regimens, such as keto, while others insist on low-fat, high-carb diets. With so many conflicting opinions and so much of details to know about the type of food we should eat, it can be challenging to determine the best approach for your health and well-being.

There is no perfect diet that should be followed solely based on what someone else tells you. Yes, there are basic guidelines for the amount of food and nutrition we need on the daily basis in the form of protein, carbs, fats and fiber and a lot more of micronutrients as well but not everyone requires the same amounts of everything.

The food we consume is significantly influenced by factors such as its availability and cost. It's essential to consider factors such as personal health goals, cultural and demographic preferences, and budget constraints when making dietary decisions.

And whatever we chose to go ahead with, we must remember that moderation is the key and excess of everything is bad, even if it is considered a healthy choice.

It is also important to figure it out early because much of what we know about our food today may not be true and could simply be what we have been made to believe for generations.

Our current food choices are often influenced by our past knowledge and the information presented to us by marketing companies. While these beliefs may have become ingrained in our belief system, it's important to recognize that not all of it is accurate or truthful.

Also, the convenient availability of processed fast food, loaded with various additives to excite the taste buds but offering little to no nutritional value, poses a problem that must be addressed at the individual level. While such food options may always be accessible, it ultimately falls on each person to decide what to consume and what to avoid for their health and well-being.

The relationship with food defines us in a way. And two different people can look at the same plate and see two different things.

An athlete may see it as all fat, carbs and a lot of calories and could want something else that can add more value and nutrition to the meal while someone addicted to fast food wouldn't give it a second thought before consuming it.

There is also a shocking amount of sugar hiding in our food. It's in everything, sometimes smaller in a quantity that doesn't taste as sweet as for us to be able to detect it and sometimes in extreme quantities in soft drinks and sweetened beverages. and all of it adds up to a huge consumption of it during a complete day.

A lot of what you find in those fast-food joints, though looks Instagram worthy, is mostly stripped of any nutritional value. So even though you could eat them when you're hungry, it isn't adding anything to the nutritional profile of the body. In other words, it could get you through the day, but it needs to change.

With time it has become more important to be able to read the labels that inform the contents of the ingredients of a package and know the details of what we consume in our daily lives. And once you start to learn to read it, it would only come as a shock. For the difference between what you were made to believe, and the reality would be hard to fathom.

That energy drink that you've been consuming has dangerous amounts of sugar in it.

That tomato Ketchup that has very little amounts of tomatoes in it. It's more of just flavour enhancers and sugar that makes it taste the way it does.

That brown bread is brown because of the colours added to it and not because it's all wheat.

And it becomes even more dangerous when you realise that what you eat also has a major effect on your mindset on an immediate basis. What goes inside you controls most of how you behave and think on the outside.

The current healthcare system operates on a cure model, addressing issues only after they have arisen due to our lifestyle choices. However, raising awareness about the consequences of our food choices is a way to shift to a prevention model, where we don't wait until we are sick to seek solutions.

Identifying what's beneficial and harmful to us, understanding their potential consequences, and exploring alternatives should be the skill everyone learns and develops early on. And it's strange that something this important isn't included in our current education system.

With kids, we can only manage this situation by setting an example and adopting a healthy lifestyle and habits, eating foods that provide value, and rejecting those we know are harmful. It's about making choices we won't regret in the long term, especially when we're at the point of no return. This includes outright rejecting empty calories in any form that have no nutritional value at all

As they say "Eat your food as medicine or later you will have to eat your medicines as food '

And the cost of poor habits is far greater than just money. No amount of exercise, regardless of its intensity or consistency, can outweigh bad food choices. We need to invest time in learning what to eat and what not to eat, understanding what's good, what's bad, and what has no value in terms of nutrition.

Conscious decisions about the quantity and quality of food are paramount, as any changes you expect in your body and mind are largely influenced by what you consume and when you consume it. By making mindful food choices, you can control compulsive eating behaviour and random weight gain cycles."

If you can't find time, then you need to go back to planning your day again and make time for the priorities.

"If you can just take out one hour from your day for your health and assume that your normal day consists of just 23 hours for everything else each single day for the next 1 year, you would not want to go back to a normal 24-hour day ever again."

Many individuals who exercise regularly also make conscious decisions to eat healthy diets, understanding that their efforts in one area complement those in others. Improvements in one aspect of life often lead to a desire to improve in others, as everything is interconnected. By dedicating more time to productive activities, having less time doesn't negatively impact the rest of the day.

Though it seems difficult at the outset, once you dedicate yourself to the schedule and have enough motivation to keep it going for the first few weeks, it starts to become addictive due to how good you start to feel after that workout. When you start to notice the changes in your body and start feeling more confident it's pretty hard to go back to the previous normal inactive ways of life.

The lose weight and get fit quick schemes are a fad and will leave you nowhere but if you are willing to change your lifestyle, follow some simple rules you can stay ahead of your game.

Lifestyle

Is Age really just a number?

It can be, as long as you stay fit to do the things you like and don't let it influence your mindset towards life

But if you won't do anything about it. Everything that can go wrong will go wrong, as stated by Murphy's Law. The state of normal, which otherwise isn't given much value, is the state we yearn for most when we are unwell.

Also, progress is slow, and the loss of the effort that you put into your body happens much faster after a certain age. The gains that follow a year of discipline can be wiped out with just a month of inactivity and bad eating habits. Starting all over again takes a lot of motivation and reason. It's like an invisible force working against us in the reverse direction at all times.

But since it's an unavoidable phenomenon shared by everybody on the planet, you can do nothing but accept the fact that you will obviously lose your looks, strength and relevance in society with age.

The approvals and rejections, the feedback we worried about long back when were more relevant and useful, had a lot of friends and people around us, the hustle, the ambitions all of it gives way to calm and routine after a time when you've seen it all.

But there will be times when we miss the people and relationships we had before. That is why we say, 'the good old days,' as we miss the carefree moments, the company, and the behaviour of our parents or children at that point in time.

How do some people live longer and healthier while others look much older and weaker than their actual age?

When you see a person looking much younger or older than their age, it has a lot to do with their genetics, but it's mostly influenced by what and how much they eat, how they move, and the small conscious choices and decisions they've made along the way.

It is mostly because of the lifestyle and routine they follow, the food they eat and how they move. But what do we exactly need to do to be able to stick to the process to achieve the desired results?

The Netflix documentary 'Living to 100 'Examines the areas of the world with the highest life expectancy. The ways to live a longer and healthier life as per the people who are already in their nineties and 100's has more to do with what they eat and how they move than anything else. No processed food, very little sugar and regular movement in the form of domestic work or community service was the best takeaway we could get from their life stories.

And more of what they had to say was about the importance of a close-knit family and society, the purpose of life and the mindset towards it. Also, to always have something to look forward to and execute when they wake up every day.

And though it isn't merely about living a substantially longer life, it surely is important for everyone to live a healthy one while sailing through it.

Life is Not that short to ignore what matters the most, your health.

If it was that short, there wouldn't be any need to worry about anything at all. And we could've lived it doing and eating whatever we wanted.

But the only way to live well and experience all of what is on offer in life is to stay fit to do it.

Some people are motivated by competition and some by fear. And some by the zest for life.

Some people only take up fitness when forced to by a doctor and told that it's necessary for their further survival.

This is a long-term game, and only if you stick to it, the later years of life will continue to give you the joy a good life promises. Otherwise, ageing could prove to be a rather painful experience, with your body bearing the brunt of your callousness during the years when it was possible to build muscle and immunity

What you do today will last until your end of days and will also decide how you spend most of them. It's a choice between popping pills every day just to perform the very basic functions or living your life doing the things you love.

Giving time to your body and the mind is the single best continuous investment you could ever make. Also owing to the fact that the better state of it also affects all other important aspects of life and decides whether you are living your life or just getting through it.

When you are fit mentally and physically it's easy to feel the passion for life and happiness and a sense of fulfilment. And when you start to do that, no age is an old age or a stage where you cannot keep up the spirit of life and what it promises.

It's then when it becomes just a number that doesn't even matter.

You feel more confident about yourself, want to learn new things, meet new people and spend more time with loved ones. You develop the ability to deal with stress and the mind starts to see more of the positives than otherwise.

Don't wait for that warning from your doctor. Start now for a better tomorrow. Not for anyone else but just for You.

"If You are busy, Make time. If you are stuck, sort your priorities."

We don't get to choose our good and bad moments or the problems that come our way. All we can choose is to stay our course while all of this happens.

There is no way you could be happy with all the success at the cost of your health, even if you have all the money in the world. It would still be worth nothing at all.

It's a time when being young at heart alone is not enough; being young in body and mind is equally important to pursue what the heart desires. It may seem difficult to start but once you do, a healthy lifestyle is more addictive than everything else combined.

Let your journey set an example for the kids and old alike.

At the end, you will see that it was all worth more than it seemed at the start.

✳ ✳ ✳

11

Politics

Is democracy an illusion? Probably.

But there is always a difference between the best and the best possible.

And even if we do control who we can chose, is it entirely based on what we believe and want or is it rather based on what we are made to believe by continuously feeding us related and biased information on all forms of media?

Politics remains the favourite subject of discussion for people in every nook and corner, and it is also something about which everyone holds an opinion. In favour or against but seldom neutral in nature.

More so when there are elections approaching. Every group is divided into discussions in favour of the candidates and the party they believe would be better for their city or the country at large. The conversations are sometimes logical and more often emotional and ideological, in which people are even ready to ignore the candidate in favour of a certain party they support.

There seems to be a much bigger market for the extremes of anything. When it comes to politics, neutral is boring and uninteresting. Normal discussions struggle to find an audience, and it's considered more of an entertainment when it's shown in an aggressive way to promote sensationalism most of the times.

While no one likes to listen to the wise side of things, some have been able to make careers out of always finding the shortcomings or the negatives of someone and something. Since it's always difficult and a lot of hard work to contribute to the truth and easier to find fault with it.

And with the intolerance that has become a norm these days, people find it challenging to accept views and beliefs contrary to their own and it's like walking that tightrope where we always have to be careful and politically correct about what we speak in public especially among the people with various beliefs. But for people who seek to garner more attention, their views merely need to provoke the emotions of many people and any attention may be good or bad, but it does help you get noticed for sure.

With frequent news and views about politicians, common people now have more insight into their lives than ever before. Their professional as well as personal lives are in the public domain now, which also makes them an easy target of critical views about how and what they should be doing at different times. They are held accountable for every single thing they say, which many times is twisted to create controversies.

People expect their leaders to be honest, sober, and idealistic, and if not that, at least the politically correct version of all of it.

And whenever they do or say even a little wrong, they are taken to task and asked for answers even if it's about something in their personal capacity and unrelated to governance at large.

But still, people everywhere have short memories. There have been a lot of politicians who have gotten away with blunders and frauds when in power. Even if found guilty, the lethargic legal process provides them enough time to feast on their illegally earned gains until they are rendered irrelevant to the system.

Sometimes we discuss the comparison of one country with another regarding law and order, the happiness index, pricing of fuel, freedom of expression, and choice. However, that's akin to comparing two completely unrelated entities at best.

The current standing of a country and the allocation of its resources depend on its population, location, overall foreign currency reserves, the natural resources it possesses, among other factors, both directly and indirectly.

Comparing what is happening and what is possible in one country to another doesn't make sense. For instance, one country might achieve peace easily due to not sharing the border with difficult neighbours, let alone multiple ones. And when a country which does need to safeguard the borders from the aggressive neighbours, a lot of resources and budget allocations go towards guarding the borders of the country in such situations, which otherwise could have been utilised for other useful purposes.

Some countries may have strategic locations suited for world trade, a few may have more natural resources than others. Some countries may embrace democracy and religious freedom while others may not. And not everywhere in the world do people have the right to choose and enjoy free speech. Some countries will have better infrastructure and medical facilities while others may not capture the world's interest at all.

It's entirely futile to compare and expect the replication of a certain aspect of a country to happen in another. Even if it is possible, executing it may lead to significant changes in the allocation and development of other sectors.

Although all countries share diplomatic relationships with each other, it's seldom possible that they have the interest of the other at the heart of their policy. It's a two-way street where everyone has to be of some use to the other to maintain its relevance. It's not always the case that the political utility of something remains constant for every country at all times.

Similarly, when political parties compare the decisions and policies of previous governments taken at different times in history, it makes very little sense.

Yes, there could have been mistakes that carry forward to this day, but it's not always certain that the decisions made at that point weren't well thought-out. It's just that the end result didn't turn out as planned owing to various scenarios that may not have been in anyone's control.

An example of this remains the response of countries to the Covid Pandemic. All countries and their governments were taken aback by its intensity. It was something that no one had ever seen before, let alone be prepared for anything like it, and when it happened, chaos ensued.

People wanted to go home but couldn't travel; medical facilities weren't enough, and fear gripped the world as it could have been the end of the world if it wasn't contained and with all of this the world came to a masked halt.

What followed in the next two months was that every country struggled, with some facing more significant challenges than others but it was a difficult period for all of them. Some have not yet completely recovered from the disastrous economic effects of it, and some never will.

When we look back at it, the Indian government is still blamed by a whole lot for mishandling it, where a lot of people lost their lives due to the non-availability of medical facilities and drugs. After the quarantine guidelines and the unavoidable lockdown followed, people even faced difficulties while travelling back to their hometowns during what was intended to be a travel ban to prevent further interstate spread of the infection.

And when this ordeal finally ended for the world, the countries with the highest approval rating for handling the pandemic well were Singapore and Sweden, followed by others.

But could the same level of response that these countries managed could have been possible in India?? Or the difference in the population and the sheer size of the country was a major factor in not being able to handle it that well or to the same extent that those countries did.

No government would've wanted to manage it any less than a perfect way, save lives and minimise discomfort, it's just that the best possible didn't prove to be the best this time.

Comparisons in situations at par do make sense, but when the involved situations and scenarios are completely different, how do we determine who handled it the best and who mishandled it.

Since everyone was caught off guard at that moment, handling a panic and fear-stricken population of 1.4 billion people sounds like an impossible task. Some due to scarcity of resources, some due to the lack of preparation, and a lot for the fear of the unknown that was to follow if all of it didn't stop.

A lot of discussions followed, done by experts, politicians, and critics who took the government to task for its mishandling of the whole situation. Not all of the positive efforts were showcased and only those incidents where things went wrong were highlighted to criticise the efforts being made.

Could others who suggested that it should've been handled better could have handled it better if they were in power?

Opposition factions create chaos, shouting their hearts out when fraudulent deals or discussions are exposed to reap political gains. However, the narrative soon fizzles out or gets lost in the legal process, and everyone goes quiet, waiting for a fresh and new opportunity.

Earlier, the modus operandi of the government and authorities was hidden to a large extent, and not everyone was aware of what was happening behind the scenes. But now, every single person with some kind of authority has to be mindful of the prying eyes of media cameras and citizen journalists, as there is a camera in every hand, and any instance of secrecy isn't as sacred as it used to be.

While this invasion of privacy or the right to information given to the common people has caused much heartburn to those with ill intentions, it also has made them a lot more accountable to the public.

And while this constant scrutiny always keeps them on their toes, it's also a hindrance in terms of performing their duties. Every decision has two sides to it, where even a decision taken for good will also have some negative aspects, and while the positive outcomes are largely noticed as the duty of those in power, the negatives catch the attention of the naysayers who try to bring it up at every possible place for people to notice that they have been wronged.

Some decisions are also based on the probability of their success and though may have been taken with the help of the best minds and calculations, they may or may not yield good results due to some unexpected random event.

Even if they do, they still leave a negative impact on a community or a sector since not all decisions taken can be beneficial for everyone in total.

Manipulation

The word is everywhere, and maybe you are being manipulated on this very day and moment itself into believing something you did not, as of now. It could be either through the content on social media or the conventional sources of information like newspapers and television news and debates. While all of it is made to appear neutral, it generally isn't.

The real neutral is boring, doesn't benefit anybody and has no takers. Doesn't create enough following for not being exciting enough to generate extreme emotions and responses.

And if we are to be convinced into believing something, it has to come with a scenario to which we could connect to, feel emotional about, and believe that could happen to us as well sooner or later. It's going on every single moment, and we are falling prey to it, again mostly not due to our fault but that's how vulnerable we are to situations and narratives.

All of what the media shows is not inherently neutral or reported as it is. The bias is visible but not evident. Also, in the competition of always being the first one to break the news, the verification process suffers, and a lot of fake narratives and first-hand false reports are aired by even the most prominent channels sometimes.

The same news or event can be shown in different ways on different channels with some added narrative depending on how they want their viewers to think of it. The media has the power to shape public perception, potentially portraying someone as a hero or a zero based on selective or even non-existent facts

The thin line between the right and wrong information has blurred even more, and what you are made to see may not always be the reality but a planned operation of sorts to create an image that suits the majority view of how the scenario, or a person should be. Pointing out only the positives of anything and comfortably leaving the negatives out of the narrative and continuously feeding us that information day in and day out via various sources is what gets the job done.

Deliberate projections and concealing of facts in favour and against have become a norm and are used whenever the opportunity arises to make the most of it.

And with the speed at which the news and data spreads on social media apps, it's becoming increasingly tough for the media companies or anyone else to verify each and every piece of information that's being posted.

To add to it, the end user is gullible to consider what's received and seen on the internet as true until proven wrong, as there is no means of verifying it. More so if the information matches the ideology of the receiver, the confirmation bias instantly suggests the mind to believe it and forward to other people to spread it more.

As they say, elections and wars are lost or won on the internet now, by making people believe what you want them to. The stronger someone's media game, the better perspective it can create in its favour.

The tools of political warfare have taken a new dimension with the social media. It refers to the strategic use of social media platforms to influence public opinion, shape and push political narratives, and ultimately impact political outcomes.

And for the time being social media has become the most effective tool to create bias and beliefs in the minds of the people, to further the agendas and propagate the narratives based on that and to sometimes spread misinformation to create doubt in the minds of people. And though all of it is much short of the conventional war, it's still enough to cause a whole lot of trouble.

Bots and fake accounts are also often used to amplify false narratives to make them appear more relevant and widespread than they actually are. Data analytics is used to calculate the preference of people regarding a certain situation and demographic after which they are shown sponsored posts on these platforms based on those preferences.

Most political campaigns have a detailed social media strategy in place and whether we choose to believe it or not, we are being manipulated every way into believing somethings which in turn moulds how and who we vote to power.

All aspects and decisions always comprise of two sides, one right and one wrong. No action or policy can be right or wrong in absolute terms. It just has to be right for those who need it more and not much wrong for those who can make do without it.

And if some people only choose to always see the wrong side of everything, while neglecting the right, it's more probable that they are doing it intentionally to malign those involved.

It would always be good to have a balanced point of view and debate, but it appears that many people present their biased views sans any logic just to vent out their frustration and in turn contribute to the absurdity reigning around.

If you have a well-calculated, fact-checked view on something, there will always be someone who can undermine it with whataboutery. Instead of addressing your logical arguments, the other side might deflect by comparing your views to a past event, often in a negative light. This is a common tactic in political debates and discussions on important decisions.

But while we argue a lot of times as to why a leader is better than the other, the process, the discussion loses its sanity and takes the path of unwanted chaos and mentions of historical misdeeds and failures.

The comparisons of governments are inevitable, and while everyone in opposition claims the system is being mismanaged by those in power, it's more or less the same when the other party gets a chance to govern the nation.

There are people who find fault with whatever the government does either by nature or under a propaganda, and always seem to have suggestions on how it should've been done differently after the event has happened if the outcomes fall short of perfection.

How can it be that everything that has been done is wrong? Is there no room for praise when things go right or does only the vicious criticism for what has gone wrong hold value for those on the opposing side?

It's like people saying a country isn't safe to live in anymore but also not wanting to go to safer countries, it's more like being politically correct in what they say but not connecting it to what they actually do.

Everyone blames industrialisation, urbanisation, fossil fuels for the pollution but keeps consuming and using the products that result in more of it. Everyone advocates saving trees but wants to have the best of wooden furniture and products for their office and home without realising that even their individual existence for every minute on this planet is adding to the carbon footprint of the world one way or the other.

But if everyone is guilty of something, is no one guilty of anything? Probably yes, at least to themselves.

Corruption

Corruption is considered normal now, as it seemingly has always been, and you cannot do a thing about it. It has become an inherent part of the system but sometimes the magnitude of it and reasons behind it may feel wrong and unwanted.

It's a basic human trait and given the opportunity and inclination, everyone indulges in it at different stages of life.

We just choose to unsee it in its various forms and sometimes turn a blind eye to it as we hesitate to acknowledge our involvement in it.

There can be variable levels of it in different countries depending on the strict laws and accountability systems, but achieving a state of zero corruption seems unattainable.

The term refers to the abuse of power for private gain. However, as its commonly used, it's not only related to the governments, regulatory bodies, or even private organisations; it remains to be a basic trait of all of us, imbibed within.

And people in their individual capacities often bend rules on a daily basis whenever there is an opportunity to do so without anyone noticing. Sometimes these actions are unknowingly done, and even though there isn't a level to which an exchange can be called an objectionable level of corruption, any magnitude of it remains to be a contribution to the overall index of corruption anyway.

It remains a basic trait of all of us, and even some of the most virtuous have had to indulge in it when there was no other way out or also if they could gain out of it without anyone realising it.

More the number of rules and compliances to execute some process, the more it becomes prone to corruption and prone to more people thinking of ways to bypass the tedious and impractical methods opting for easier and less expensive and comfortable alternatives.

Most people, when given that place of power and authority which they blame for being extremely corrupt, probably would also have to handle it the same way as it's always been, even if they didn't want to do it, in the first place.

It's the system that makes you behave a certain way, and it is how life, people, and politics work in sync with each other. And sometimes if not for your personal gains, you have to behave like all others to remain a part of the system.

For you still need to be in the system to do the good that you want to, and it may very well mean doing a few things you would not have otherwise. And while it's impossible to change the system and how the world works, the basic tenets of it are fixated in a way humans are hardwired to behave in chaos. On the flip side, it's still feasible and easier for the system and people involved to change you if you want to stay involved in it.

There will always be those out of power making promises of solving all this, the truth is that no one can solve everything. And even if they can, it's a truth that one solution breeds new problems when there are so many people and elements involved.

The truth is that there will always be disparity and inequality in the world, there will always be corruption, crimes and unemployment, the economic growth of a country could never be equally shared with all its population. There will be politics based on caste, religion, freebies since it's only the people who respond to that positively.

There will be inflation when there is growth and job losses when there is a slowdown. The rags to riches stories will also accompany the riches to rag ones.

Industries will shut down, companies will go bankrupt, and banks will go bust; there will also be huge loan defaults when there is a subprime crisis in real estate, an asset class that has been considered ever stable in recent times.

No government can provide jobs to all the aspirants, and no number of jobs can keep pace with a large population; pandemics and natural disasters will keep happening, and with more people, there will be more pollution and trash and chaos in the world.

All of this is cyclical, and this is how the world economy and nature work, and it's no different for any country or location. There are a whole lot of us on the planet to keep contributing to the chaos that has become a part of the system.

It's all of us, a lot of us. We are the crowd, and we are the ones that create situations that cannot be solved, and it will need a super villain like Thanos to make disappear at least half of us for things to start to get better.

Moreover, so when we are also allowed to have an opinion and share our views on anything and everything as well. And while it's always good to point out the problem, it may also help to suggest and do our small bit towards the solutions.

And yes, there could possibly be someone someday good enough, who would know how to solve all the above problems mentioned and sync all the energy and resources in the positive direction and create a utopian society where everyone is happy, treated the same, where all contingencies are taken care of, and all situations are handled with utmost precision.

'For we would all like to vote for the best man, but he is never a candidate.' Someone said.

And even if he is, and we could choose him to do what we think he will be able to, he may still never be able to survive the system and may end up just like everyone else.

12

The Future

Make no mistake, we are at an inflection point.
Not in a distant future, but if you look close enough the
revolution is already upon us.

Consider a scenario, if people in the 1950's were told of the current day's technologies like the smartphones, flying machines, self-driving electric vehicles, the information and infinite data available in an instant, would they have been able to believe it or even give a thought to it being remotely possible. Not really.

Then what leads us to believe that only what we can think of right now will be the reality of the next few decades?

Every step forward is a bridge to the future that we imagine and also to that we do not.

Now with more computing power to process all that available data and the ability to derive solutions based on them, the technological advances have become so fast that it can be assumed that the changes in the next 2-3 decades will easily surpass the net of all technological breakthroughs there have been for all of human existence. All of it may sound far-fetched but most of us will probably live to see the transition as it promises to be here soon.

There is a chance that within the next 10-20 years Artificial Intelligence will surpass the human intelligence quotient and with it has the potential to significantly impact all aspects of human existence while promising possibilities that had not been even imagined till a few years ago.

Soon enough with the help of Ai, humans may be able to increase their productivity exponentially, solve the unsolved till now and may even be able to live longer, solve most, if not all of human disability and diseases, the possibilities remain endless.

Brain-computer interface tech companies like Neuralink are also working on integrating the power of human mind with Ai by planting a device wherein the learning and execution capabilities of both entities can be merged to operate at a much higher efficiency levels.

If it works out we may no longer have to even speak to convey what we want to, may have the exact data on the body's reaction to whatever we consume, learn and execute complex theories in an instant with the direct data transfer between the brain and digital devices.

With all of this, it's quite possible that AI may also replace most of the jobs that exist right now though creating a lot of new ones with it with a prerequisite that new workforce knows the applications of AI in all work formats.

Although all of this will take some time to have a significant impact on our daily lives, but when it does, we better hope that it turns out the way we imagine it now. And since it's inevitable, just the hope of the transition leaning more towards the positive side than the negative would help the world embrace the AI development in a better way.

And irrespective of whether we remain to be excited or anxious about Ai and machine learning, it has already started to show up everywhere. And as the time passes the machines are getting smarter with every moment.

But that's not what it's about, not assuming how it's going to shape up and not how to deal with it when it does. It's About what we as humans can do to keep ourselves relevant in a world where the AI finds its application in almost everything we have ever done and have the potential to do going forward.

And when we discuss staying relevant, it could only be about involving next generation technologies and possibilities in our education system. and the use of current knowledge systems incorporating the applications of AI and then finding the Solutions to existing problems with it. The solution of human inefficiencies through AI will involve integration of the old and the new, but alongside, we also need to make efforts to monitor the progress closely and keep the functioning of AI in check.

Also, as every solution breeds new problems, with a future where there could be infinite productivity and accuracy with the advent of AI, one question still remains unanswered.

If the machine would be able to do all that humans can do, what would we do?

Though AI may not replace humans completely but humans with AI will replace humans without it or at least without any knowledge of it.

And it's because of this that we need to reinvent our conventional education system. Take every single aspect and subject of it and then add the applications of machine learning and AI to the content.

Since whatever is being taught in the system right now, the theories, calculations, executions and the cognitive tasks would soon be done by machines with much better accuracy and speed. And if we continue to educate our young like this there is soon going to be an unemployable generation not knowing what to do with all that redundant knowledge.

Also, because the AI would be able to consume and process historical and real time data of infinite proportions in an instant while it would be impossible for the human mind to receive and make sense of anything even close to that.

The intelligent machines and algorithms will take away a lot of jobs since they will be able to harness all the available data and execute and solve even most of the tasks given to it at much faster speeds.

And if there was ever a time when the education system of the world was to change, it is now. The current one is useful only to imbibe discipline and develop learning skills, but whatever we are taught in all those years would not remain useful in the real world for most people in the next few decades.

Yes, the current education system does gets you there till an age where you are able to decide better for yourself given whatever you have studied and the subjects you've had exposure to may find its application in your future endeavours, but the process should stop taking this long since the kids today are smarter than any generation has ever seen.

It isn't like they were born and developed a better brain and cognitive abilities, it's more of the early exposure to the information and learnings. Also with what they see and try to replicate from social media and the internet and with the derived motivation from the competition they have in the form of their equals and sometimes much better peers, all of it makes them execute, experiment and explore more.

The Question is "Can the AI also change the way we learn …and find its application in the better education model that we are looking for?"

Probably it can.

The biggest problem anywhere in the education model is the availability of teachers that are qualified and capable enough, the student to teacher ratio and the cost of learning from these teachers.

AI can help in providing virtual experts in all subjects to all institutions and since everyone potentially could have their own personal teacher, in this case the students can decide the subjects amongst the available options, take lessons anywhere, anytime and can even have the immediate feedback and queries solved by the teacher.

In later stages of its development, the experience could be akin to having a personal teacher and mentor available to a student at a much lower cost than it is right now.

With the help of augmented reality, the experience of learning and execution can be elevated to life-like proportions All of this could be done while being accountable to the institution for verifying and grading the results.

But what if technology leaves the education system redundant and whatever if to be learned could be learned just by transferring the data to the integrated chip in the brain.

Recall a famous scene from the movie 'The Matrix' where Trinity instantly learns to fly a helicopter. If brain-computer interface tech advances far enough, such rapid acquisition of complex skills could very well become a reality.

The AI engines, though still only able to think in a limited capacity, are being used to write movie Scripts, generate original lyrics and tunes, as virtual assistants, in self-driving cars. And make no assumptions, real people who were still in denial about the advent of Ai are losing real jobs because of it.

Also because of the fact that it would require much less effort and money to execute a lot of tasks with the help of intelligent machines than with real people.

But what makes the machines better than humans? To begin with, being more accurate at everything they will be able to do, the machines will also be more productive. No time limits, no calling in sick, and to add to it, no training and time required for knowledge transfer, just straightforward instructions and execution.

Consider the example of a Chess Playing Software, it could just start with the rules of the chess and use historical data to assess all the previous chess matches ever recorded and use machine learning and play and practise with itself, try different moves and strategies and learn while doing that.

What's astonishing is that it could manage to learn and execute all that a human mind would take several years to decode and grasp in just a few hours or even less than that in the future. With more computing power it may just take seconds for any system to learn any process with whatever amounts of data is available.

A human mind will never be able to win that kind of a contest and wherever it's a matter of accuracy, speed and reduced costs, more efficient systems will continue to take over as they always have.

But like every piece of tech could be used for better, it could also have its negatives, and in this case it's already becoming evident.

Deepfake applications can generate fake audio and videos of any person, AI systems can be used to create fake news and narratives by creating life-like pictures of someone not even involved.

By showing an influential person doing and saying something that has not been said or done, it has the potential to create a lot of dangerous scenarios as people would hardly be able to spot the fake ones from the real and since any piece of data spreads like wildfire thanks to social media and messaging apps, the potential harm that can be caused by such manipulated information and content is multifaceted, ranging from influencing mass public opinion and actions to eroding the credibility of institutions.

There have been a lot of instances where the tech made to ease our lives solved an aspect of it but ended up creating a lot more chaos with it. Over time, more instances of misinformation engines will emerge making it increasingly difficult to distinguish between real and fake information.

Since too much of everything is bad, it remains to be the same with the use of technology as well. Moreover so, if it continues to replace human interaction in society as it already begun to do.

Can there be artificial emotions and responses based on that, exactly like there is artificial intelligence?

Not really the natural ones, but probably the calculated ones being able to display anger, surprise, joy, sadness as per the situations and data received.

The words spoken by the machines could be estimated to have an exact sync with the feelings of who it's interacting with. The responses, in some cases, could also be programmed to be exactly the same as what the person in conversation with it wants to hear or feel at that time.

And precisely that is a substantial part of the problem.

When the machines have the ability to do that, would there be good and bad machines like there are people?

And would all of it affect their decision-making algorithms exactly like it happens with humans when there are emotions involved. Probably not, because that is what they are exactly being made to avoid but that's only when everything goes exactly as planned which it seldom does when there are so many variables involved

Even if there can be a certain behaviour set in to respond in certain situations, will it be enough to form deeper connections. Since it's the human interaction that is the basis of all emotions and deeper relationships. But with technology taking over every aspect of our lives, who is to say that this one will remain unaffected by it.

And when the AI develops emotions and somewhat meaningful interactions, calculated or natural, will the humans continue to need the humans?

Technology does not promise to fulfil all the emotional needs of humans like genuine connection, love and stable relationships but when these are not being fulfilled in the real world, a switch to AI for at least a partial feeling of it would be imminent. Where people may rely on tech for emotional companionship as well, one where they wouldn't be judged and can customise the needs and preferences that would make the machine companion behave and also not behave a certain way.

The major impact that AI promises to have on the world would be mainly due to its ability to make informed and unbiased decisions devoid of impulsive emotions. And if its emotional quotient gets in the way of that, then the machines would prove to be no better than us. Or if only there could be a switch to turn on and off the emotions of machines if they manage to develop some.

Humans? When a machine is asked about it.

What about them? It may say.

Imagine waking up on a 2040 Morning. Electric Air taxis, Robots running around, machines talking to each other.

That could be the time when humanity has reached the AI singularity where the machines and technology have surpassed human intelligence and control. Algorithms have cognitive capabilities now and can self-replicate to create an exponential cycle of technical advancements.

Do we even matter in the scheme of that future??

Or it will all be eventually taken over by the AI machines while treating humans as a liability whose views and authority won't matter anymore.

What happens to countries and religions then?? Will there be any left or the supreme Ai machine will unify all of them to form a single entity governed by it.

All of it may sound like a far-fetched doomsday scenario or a conspiracy theory at best. Let's hope that it remains that way.

The raw computing power that we possess right now is beyond belief but it's a waste until put to proper use. Exactly like a human brain which has infinite potential to solve cognitive tasks, but we rarely use it to its full potential for various reasons and distractions.

AI systems promise to solve a lot of problems when they reach the point of singularity where they will probably be able to innovate without any human interference.

Until now, humans have been the most intelligent group the planet has ever seen. But what will happen when there will be two such entities? And what's when one becomes far more of that than the other. Only time will tell.

The technology used until now has been inherently neutral and the consequences both positive and negative have been correlated with how it is used by the people.

Though the AI machines or algorithms for the time being do not execute the wishes of their own, it's learning from the infinite amount of historical as well as the real time data that is being generated on various platforms by millions of people around the world.

Intelligent machines that can learn and understand from patterns, make recommendations and decisions. Sounds fun for now for sure.

Though it's been talked about much now the data-based Ai has been here since a long time … the search engines, the YouTube and Instagram recommendations, the ecommerce websites sites knowing what segment interests you when you search for something and then showing you ads related to that are all examples of an algorithm learning from your behaviour and propensity and showing you similar content.

The trigger for execution despite all the recommendations has always been in our hands and it would only become a problem when that final choice of decision is partially or completely is taken away by the machines.

Let's hope that it's the symbiosis of the machines and the humans that would shape the future of the planet.

The Collaboration could harness the intuition and contextual understanding of humans alongside computational power, analysis and automation capabilities of the machine and can be used in the future to achieve what neither could possibly attain on their own. If only we could know what's in the future and plan accordingly to live our lives a certain way. Since it's impossible we can only move forward to the future with a belief that everything will work out in the end like it almost always does.

Carpe Diem. Is all we can end this with.